WILL DRAFTING

DANA SHILLING

Prentice-Hall, Inc.
Englewood Cliffs, New Jersey

Prentice-Hall International, Inc., *London*
Prentice-Hall of Australia, Pty. Ltd., *Sydney*
Prentice-Hall Canada, Inc., *Toronto*
Prentice-Hall of India Private Ltd., *New Delhi*
Prentice-Hall of Japan, Inc., *Tokyo*
Prentice-Hall of Southeast Asia Pte. Ltd., *Singapore*
Editora Prentice-Hall do Brasil Ltda., *Rio de Janeiro*
Prentice-Hall Hispanoamericana, S.A., *Mexico*

© 1987 *by*
PRENTICE-HALL, INC.
Englewood Cliffs, N.J.

This publication is designed to provide accurate and
authoritative information in regard to the subject
matter covered. It is sold with the understanding that
the publisher is not engaged in rendering legal,
accounting, or other professional service. If legal
advice or other expert assistance is required, the
services of a competent professional person should be
sought.
*...From the Declaration of Principles jointly adopted by a
Committee of the American Bar Association and a Committee
of Publishers and Associations.*

Library of Congress Cataloging-in-Publication Data

Shilling, Dana.
  Will drafting.

  Includes index.
  1. Wills—United States. 2. Trusts and
trustees—United States. 3. Wills—United States—
Forms. 4. Trusts and trustees—United States—
Forms. I. Title.
KF755.S53   1987   346.7305'4   86-30265
                      347.30654

ISBN 0-13-959727-1

ABOUT THE AUTHOR: Dana Shilling is a graduate of the Harvard Law School and is a member of the New York bar who devotes herself to legal writing, editing, and language simplification. She is the author of five law-related books for the lay audience, and has worked on several legal looseleaf services, including CCH's *Business Strategies*. She is the series editor for the *Prentice-Hall Law Practice Portfolios* series.

Printed in the United States of America

What This Portfolio Can Do for You

Drafting wills and trusts can be like running through a minefield. First, you've got to find out what your client owns (and is likely to own when he or she dies), who the client wants to benefit, and who has a right to object to the client's dispositive scheme. Then you have to construct an estate plan that carries out the client's dispositive scheme, or comes as close as possible without disastrous tax consequences.

But you are not finished yet. You have to find the words that will embody the estate plan—so clearly that there is no possible ambiguity to be construed by a court, without falling afoul of various state laws, and in compliance with state laws about testamentary capacity, signature, and attestation. Will contests have turned on the interpretation of single words—and even of single punctuation marks, so you will have to be sure you pick exactly the right words.

This portfolio is designed as a guide through the minefield. Chapters one through seven are a brief guide to the drafting problems you may encounter.

- Chapter one gives some tips for effective client interviews, and discusses the forms and records you will need to keep as part of an efficient and profitable will-drafting practice.

- Chapter two deals with the general rules about revocation of earlier wills—either automatically, by operation of law (depending on state law, when a client marries, has a child, or divorces) or by the client's own action with intent to revoke.

- Chapter three deals with the formalities required of a valid formal will—how it must be signed; how it must be witnessed (and the effect of an interested witness); whether it can be self-proved; and how to use codicils effectively.

- Chapter four is a quick summary of the limits on a testator's freedom to dispose of his property however he likes—the spouse's right to elect; rights of pretermitted spouses and children (those who are not mentioned in the will—presumably because the testator forgot them, not because he or she wanted to prevent them from inheriting). This chapter also contains tips for getting around these statutes, if the testator's intent *is* to disinherit. The related topic of *in terrorem*, "no contest," clauses is also treated here.

- Chapter five deals with the procedural problems of will drafting: how to organize a will; problems of definitions; disposing of all (but not more than all) of the testator's personal property; dealing with contingencies; and the like. This chapter also contains tips for effective plain English drafting.

- Chapter six deals with the substantive issues in will drafting, for example, testamentary capacity, abatement, exoneration, apportionment of estate taxes, and simultaneous death.

- Chapter seven is a brief summary of drafting techniques for effective trusts.

The rest of the portfolio consists of short, simple wills and trust instruments, and clauses for constructing more elaborate documents.

Each clause is identified by function (for example, **Title does not vest** in a spendthrift trust). When clauses are grouped together and numbered, each numbered clause serves a different function. If there are two direct alternatives with the same function, they are assigned the same number, and separated by the word "or." If a clause is long, it is divided and each subpart is lettered (for example, 1a, b, c, and d).

Within a clause, if I suggest several alternatives, they will be separated by virgules: "to my wife/son/daughter/friend _____." Fill-in lines have been provided where necessary. The material in brackets ([ ]) is optional: for example, a requirement that the beneficiary survive the testator by a certain number of days to inherit.

I'd like to add a warning to drafters who build a new instrument out of separate clauses: check them carefully to be sure that they do not contradict each other! For instance, one clause may be designed for an irrevocable trust, another for a revocable trust; combining them may lead to litigation, or to adverse tax consequences. Also, check each clause before use—it may be written with another state's laws in mind, or based on a Code section or revenue ruling that has since been changed, or a case that has been overruled.

Finally, this portfolio, like all the portfolios in the series, includes a Table of Cases and a fifty state Table of Statutes to help you in your research (and to make it easy for you to check your particular state's requirements), and a list of resources: treatises, looseleaf services, law review and other articles, and so forth.

Contents

WILL DRAFTING FLOW CHART

This Flow Chart is a "map" of a complete will, showing the types of clauses you may wish to include, and drafting problems you may encounter.

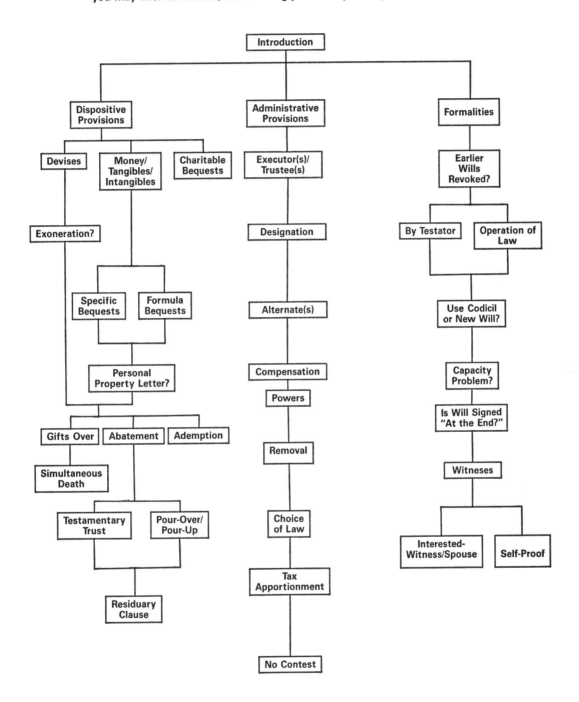

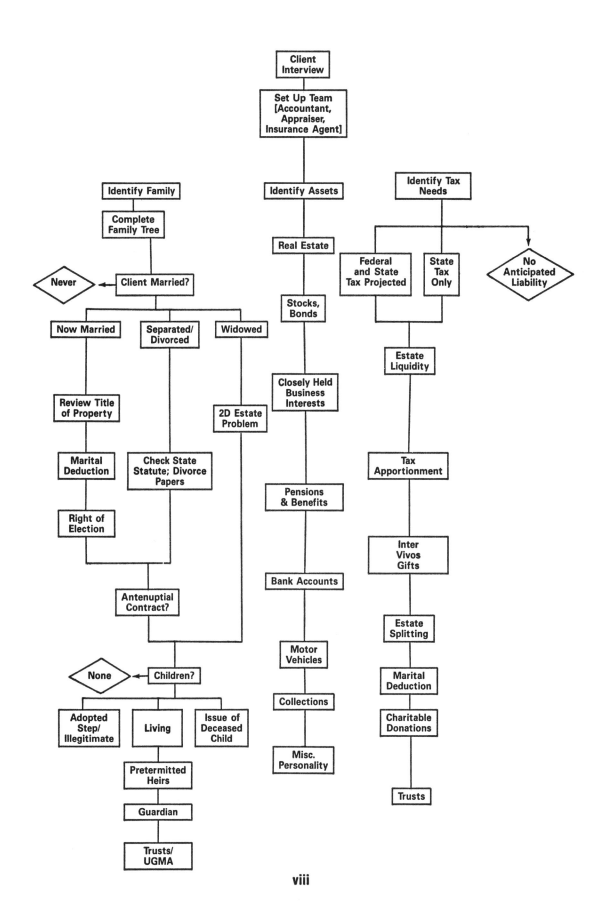

1

CLIENT INTERVIEWING AND RECORDKEEPING

Drafting a client's will is the middle step in a three-step process. First, the lawyer must get a complete and accurate picture of the client's personal and financial situations, and must create an estate plan to provide for the client's family and dispose of the client's property according to his or her wishes. The estate plan integrates the will with insurance, joint property, payable on death accounts, and nontestamentary instruments such as *inter vivos* trusts.

The second step is to draft the will itself: to comply with any formalities required by the state, effectuate the client's wishes, and make provisions for reasonable contingencies.

If the first two steps have been satisfactory to the client, the lawyer will probably be given a role (either as executor or as counsel to the executor) in probating the will and administering the estate. Other portfolios in this series will deal with the first and third steps; this portfolio contains plain English sample wills, will clauses, trusts, and trust clauses, with a discussion of common drafting problems.

In this portfolio you will find fairly simple wills for married, single, or divorced people, with or without children. There are no very complex wills involving multiple trusts. Joint wills (a single will for a married couple) and mutual wills (wills with complementary provisions, and with an express or implied agreement not to revoke the provisions in favor of the other joint testator) are not covered, based on the assumption that they create more problems than they solve. Consider the common situation in which the co-testators separate, divorce, or simply change their minds. Instead, it is a better practice for each spouse to have a separate will, without limitations on amendment or revocation.

The suggestions in this portfolio are based on some further assumptions. It is better for the client to have a formal, attested will than to die intestate (even if the client's estate plan parallels the state's scheme of intestacy). If nothing else, the existence of the will precludes any attempt to establish that a "lost" or "hidden" will creates some other scheme of disposition more palatable to the would-be will proponents. Nor will holographic wills (those admissible to probate despite the absence of some of the will formalities required by statute) be treated; there is no reason for a lawyer to prepare anything other than a formal attested will. A last assumption is that the federal estate tax on the testator's estate will be minimal or nonexistent, either because of the size of the estate or because the marital deduction is used to eliminate the tax on the first estate.

Therefore, your focus must be on developing an efficient system that allows you to assess the client's needs, research the applicable law, and draft to respond to those needs—while charging (and collecting) a fee that makes the transaction a profitable one for you. *PRACTICE TIP: Many firms with an extensive trusts and estates practice find that they can make money even if their fees for routine drafting are low—if they create a reputation for profitable estate-administration tasks.*

SETTING AND COLLECTING FEES

All of the three major fee-setting approaches are sometimes used by will drafters.

- A flat fee for interviewing a client and preparing a simple will; a higher flat fee for preparing a more complex will involving trusts, or a will plus related documents such as *inter vivos* trust and power of attorney. *PRACTICE TIP: even if you adopt this approach, accurate hourly records are a must—so you can decide if your flat fee is realistic in terms of the time you must expend and the other projects you must sacrifice. Too many lawyers set a flat fee (more or less by guesswork) and continue to charge it even though it guarantees unprofitable work, and even though clients are able and willing to pay higher fees.*

- An hourly fee for the work of interviewing, researching, and drafting. If this is your approach, make sure that you record and "capture" all the time you spend on the matter.

Will drafting includes frequent telephone calls, both from anxious clients (perhaps discussing some financial planning tip derived—accurately or not—from a magazine or radio program) and to clients to check matters not brought out during the in-office interviews or missing from the questionnaire. Will drafting also requires a high volume of correspondence, not only with the client but with state agencies to get copies of documents, with others to check facts, and so forth. ***PRACTICE TIP:*** *One way to handle this is with a highly accurate billing system that records 1/10 of an hour transactions (and a reminder to your clients that they will be billed for at least 1/10 to 1/4 of an hour for every call or letter). Another way is to charge your usual hourly rates for sustained periods of time, such as two hours of research or an hour and a half of drafting, plus a fee for each call or letter sent or received.*

- "Contingent" fees. In the will-drafting context, this means a fee measured by the expected size of the eventual estate, such as, $1 for every $1,000 of expected estate value.

Attorneys sometimes have psychological problems about charging appropriate fees for will drafting. Why? They are embarrassed by their own efficiency. As a result of practice, they can interview a client effectively (and use questionnaires and other practice aids) and find out the necessary information in a short time. Because they have drafted many wills and trusts, they have a "library" of useful forms and clauses. Because they are responsible about continuing their legal education, they are aware of recent cases, and of changes in state and federal laws affecting estate planning. When all these factors are put together, it doesn't take much time to plan the client's estate and draft the necessary forms.

Is the lawyer justified in charging hundreds or even thousands of dollars for a few hours' work? Certainly, *if* the fee fairly represents the *value* that the lawyer's services provide to the client. After all, if hours spend were the sole measure of value, clients would always be better off with an inexperienced, inefficient lawyer who would have to "invent the wheel" on every matter (and who would waste a great deal of time doing even that). Nor would lawyers have any incentive to find more efficient ways of expediting matters while still providing first-rate representation to their clients.

It has often been pointed out that the key to getting clients to pay their bills is emphasizing this value approach. Most clients do want to meet their obligations, and will pay their bills unless the severest financial hardship is involved. Experts have identified several keys to getting bills paid.

- Send out the bills promptly! Clients are more likely to pay a bill promptly when they are grateful for recently rendered services—not when the lawyer's services are only a vague memory.
- Be businesslike. Bills should be neat and clean, and clearly identify both the lawyer's services performed and any costs or disbursements involved. In this context, that probably means copying, postage, and telephone calls.
- A good bill, like a good résumé, concentrates on verbs. The verbs shows the client exactly what you have done for him or her. That is, a bill stating, "Interviewed clients Anne and Todd Richardson. Reviewed their financial

holdings. Telephoned employers to review employee benefits. Researched effect of new tax law on existing trusts. Drafted will, durable power of attorney, and *inter vivos* trust for each client," is much more impressive than one that says merely, "For services rendered," plus a fee.

WILL DRAFTING AS A PRACTICE BUILDER

A lawyer who asks the right questions often finds out that a client who asks to have a will drafted has many other pressing legal needs. The lawyer who educates the client about these needs has a good chance of being retained to handle the other matters, and of getting new clients as the original client tells other people about the lawyer's expertise and practical approach to legal problems in their real-life context.

EXAMPLE: Robert Slater (date of birth 4/30/46) comes into your office, asking that you draft his will. He is married to the former Margaret Joy Gallagher (born 7/19/51). He tells you "they" have three children. Mr. Slater is a vice-president in a family owned corporation, with a good income. His assets include a home now worth $140,000, two cars, a modest portfolio, and a great deal of stock in the (closely held) family corporation.

However, this seemingly straightforward situation is seen to be more complicated as you inquire. For one thing, only two of the children are Robert and Margaret's; the third is Margaret's son by an earlier marriage. You must explore whether he wants all three to be treated on a parity. (It is not unlikely that other members of the Slater family will object to this "outsider" getting stock in the family business; there may even be transfer restrictions on the stock.)

For another thing, Robert was also married before—and his separation agreement requires him to make provisions in his will for his ex-wife. Either he never noticed this provision in the agreement, or he neglected to mention it to you before you asked. Furthermore, he and his ex-wife have a child (who lives with her)—and who would be a "pretermitted child" if she is left out of Robert's will.

One way to handle the situation is simply to draft a will for Robert, once *all* the relevant information has been found. But a better way—both for Robert and his family, and for your reputation and prosperity as a practitioner—is to advise him of other legal steps that can be taken. You might be retained to perform some or all of these tasks:

- Drafting a will for Margaret. A good job done on Robert's and Margaret's will could bring many other family members and friends to you as clients. Furthermore, Robert and Margaret could know someone who has just qualified as executor or administrator of an estate, and who needs to hire an attorney for help with these tasks.

- Drafting durable powers of attorney and/or trusts for Robert and Margaret. These tools might be even more useful for older family members, such as Robert's father (President of the family corporation).

- Closely held corporations frequently lack a practical provision for succession. If Robert is impressed with your legal skills, you could be hired to advise the corporation about matters such as recapitalization and retirement income for the older generation managers. You might also gain the corporation as a retainer client for its routine legal matters.
- Robert and Margaret are likely to have potentially taxable estates; Robert's parents are even more likely to do so. You can advise them about estate taxes, and perhaps set up a "giving program" to reduce the taxable estate.

In short, a little probing reveals possible drafting problems in this "simple, routine" matter. Any competent lawyer would ask the right questions and avoid the malpractice traps. But an imaginative lawyer would not just carry out the client's request for a will in a competent but prosaic way. The imaginative lawyer fully explores the client's legal needs and suggests steps that can be taken to enhance the client's legal and financial position.

THE DRAFTER'S TASK

A well-drafted will disposes of exactly 100% of the testator's property that *can* pass by will. This is not quite the truism it seems. Wills can fail to express the testator's wishes, fail to meet the needs of the testator's family, create unfavorable financial and/or tax situations, or give rise to litigation for many reasons. For example,

- the will is simply unclear—bad drafting makes it impossible to understand the testator's intention, or impossible to carry it out under the relevant state laws.
- the local requirements for creating a new will or codicil, or revoking an old one, are not observed. If the mistake is the lawyer's, the probability of malpractice liability is high.
- the testator fails to dispose of all his or her willable property—perhaps because the testator's assets increased substantially between the time the will was drafted and the time of death. If there is a well-drafted residuary clause, this problem is less severe, because at least the property goes to *someone* the testator intended to benefit, although not necessarily the person the testator would have wanted to have the property if he or she had fully understood the extent of his or her property.
- the intended beneficiary dies before the testator does, and the will is not amended to compensate. If the intended beneficiary was a close relative of the testator's, most states have "anti-lapse" statutes providing that the deceased person's children take the property instead.
- the testator attempts to dispose of *more* than 100% of his or her property that can pass by will. For example, he or she may:

—leave objects that were sold, stolen, or destroyed during the testator's lifetime. This is known as *ademption*, and usually, unless the will makes provision to the contrary, the intended beneficiary is out of luck. (Many states have *non-ademption* statutes limited in their applications to certain sorts of property such as marketable securities.)

—attempt to dispose of a closely held business interest covered by a buy–sell agreement and/or transfer restrictions that provide for automatic transfer of the business interest or give some person or entity a right of first refusal in the business interest.

—attempt to dispose of joint property, unaware that the property passes by operation of law to the other joint tenant(s)

—attempt to dispose of 100% of any community property or quasi-community property owned by the testator and spouse. The general rule is that half the community property passes to the surviving spouse by operation of law, so only half can be controlled by the will of the first spouse to die. The testator may also characterize an asset as separate property when it is really community property, and vice versa.

—circumstances (for example, the testator's retirement and heavy medical expenses) reduce the estate so much that it is impossible to satisfy all debts, claims against the estate, and administration expenses and still satisfy the legacies provided in the will. Most of the states have *abatement* rules specifying the reductions to be made in legacies; however, the testator may prefer another pattern of abatement.

INTERVIEW PROBLEMS

In order to make a will, the testator must confront the inevitability of his or her own death, and must make a realistic assessment of the property he or she will own at the time of death and the obligations this property must satisfy. The testator is naturally reluctant to think about his own mortality, and the possible termination of his marriage or hostility in family relationships. The lawyer, in turn, is squeamish about asking probing questions needed to uncover the extent of the testator's estate, his or her debts, marital history and marriage plans, and the number of the testator's children (legitimate and otherwise). It may be necessary to expose business and marital failures, and to confront the client's twin fears that his or her family will be left destitute, and that he or she is worth more to the family dead than alive.

One way the lawyer can defuse the situation is to break the process of making a will into several steps, with a separate appointment for each. At the first meeting, the lawyer can get a general idea of the client's potential estate and general dispositive plans. At this meeting, the lawyer also gives the client some general information about will-making and estate planning, and a detailed questionnaire to fill out. The client completes the questionnaire at home, and mails it back to the lawyer, who uses the questionnaire and interview notes from the earlier meeting to make a preliminary draft of the will. At the second meeting, the lawyer reviews the will and the overall estate plan with the client. If the client approves of the will and plan, the will can be executed, and the client advised of the need for regular review of the will. The client should also be advised of the state law of revocation.

If the client does not approve, the will and estate plan can be modified (at least to the extent that the client's wishes are legal) and a final, brief appointment set for review of the revisions and execution of the revised will.

There are several advantages to this procedure. It educates the client about the varieties of estate planning devices available to him or her. It allows the client to complete the inventory away from the lawyer's office, minimizing the embarrassment of discussing intimate personal and financial matters, and it frees the lawyer from the clerical tasks of completing the property inventory, allowing him or her to focus on planning and legal advice. (If you have a problem with clients who delay in completing the inventory or setting up follow-up appointments, it may help to have a paralegal interview the client and complete the inventory.)

CLIENT PROPERTY INVENTORY

Note: For each item of property, use Column 1 to indicate the person you want to receive that property after you die; use Column 2 to indicate the person you want to receive that property if the person in Column 1 dies before you do.

BACKGROUND (Questions 1–10)

1. Your name:

2. Address:

3. Are you married? [ ] No [ ] Yes: spouse's name:
   Date of marriage:

4. Were you ever married before? [ ] No [ ] Yes: my marriage to
   _____ ended on _____ by [ ] his/her death [ ]
   divorce # _____ granted by the _____ Court of
   _____.

5. Do you have any children? [ ] No [ ] Yes. (Give their names and dates
   of birth):
   Do you have custody of all your children? [ ] Yes [ ] No,
   _____ has custody of _____.

6. Are any of these children adopted, step-children, or born out of
   wedlock? [ ] No [ ] Yes (explain):

7. Are your parents still alive? [ ] No (names, dates of death) [ ] Yes. (Give
   names and addresses).

8. Do you have any brothers or sisters? [ ] No [ ] Yes (give names and
   addresses).

9. Did you have any brothers or sisters who died? [ ] No [ ] Yes (give
   name, date of death, names and addresses of surviving spouse and
   children).

10. Name and address of your employer: [ ] None [ ] Self-employed.

ESTATE PLANNING INFORMATION (Questions 11–22)

11. Give a brief description, in your own words, of your general plan for your estate:

12. Do you want the insurance policies listed in Question 32 to be paid to a specific person, or to your estate? [ ] Named beneficiary [ ] Estate. NOTE: Be sure to consult your insurance agent about changing the beneficiary, if necessary.

13. Do you have a power of appointment under anybody else's will? [ ] No [ ] Yes (describe):

14. Have you made an antenuptial agreement with your spouse or intended spouse covering inheritance rights? [ ] No [ ] Yes: date: _____ description: _____
NOTE: Attach a copy of this agreement to the inventory.

15. Do you want to leave your spouse less than the statutory share explained by your lawyer? [ ] No [ ] Yes.

16. Do you plan to disinherit anyone who would be considered a natural heir? [ ] No [ ] Yes (explain):

17. Do you want a "penalty clause" disinheriting anyone who contests your will? [ ] No [ ] Yes.

18. If the estate is not large enough to pay all the legacies provided by the will, what should be done?
    [ ] Eliminate some legacies entirely, pay the rest in full
    [ ] Eliminate some legacies entirely, pay a proportion of the rest
    [ ] Reduce all legacies proportionately
    [ ] Other (explain):

19. If there are any estate or inheritance taxes, how do you want them paid:
    [ ] From the residue of the estate
    [ ] From this source:
    [ ] Have all the legatees pay proportionately
    [ ] Other (explain):

20. If anyone inherits property subject to a mortgage, lien, or security interest, how do you want it handled?
    [ ] Have the executor pay off the mortgage, etc. (reducing the residuary estate)
    [ ] The property should be inherited subject to the mortgage, etc.

21. If you and your spouse both die while your children are minors, who do you want to act as their personal guardian? As the guardian of their property?

22. Have you made any gifts that you want treated as advancements (subtracted from the donee's share of the estate)?
    [ ] No [ ] Yes (explain):

PROPERTY (Questions 23–44)

23. Do you own a house, co-op, or condominium used as your principal residence?
[ ] No [ ] Yes (describe; give address; approximate value; and outstanding balance and terms of any mortgage).

24. If yes, is it:
[ ] In your name only
[ ] Tenancy in common with:
[ ] Joint tenancy with:
[ ] Tenancy by the entirety with your spouse

25. Do you own a vacation home or income-producing real estate?
[ ] No [ ] Yes (describe; give address; type of property; approximate value; any co-owners; balance and terms of any mortgate)

26. To whom do you want to leave any interest in your real estate that you can pass by will?
Column 1   Column 2

27. Do you own an automobile? [ ] No [ ] Yes (describe it; give its title, approximate value, balance and terms of any auto loan)
Column 1   Column 2

28. Do you own a boat? [ ] No [ ] Yes (describe as for automobile)
Column 1   Column 2

29. Do you own valuable jewelry? [ ] No [ ] Yes (describe, including insurance coverage)
Column 1   Column 2

30. Do you own stocks, bonds, or other securities? [ ] No [ ] Yes (attach list, indicating if they are in sole or joint name)
Column 1   Column 2

Do you own stock in a closely held business? [ ] No [ ] Yes (describe, including transfer restrictions, buy-sell agreements, and other limitations on free transfer)
Column 1   Column 2

31. Do you have any CDs or money market accounts? [ ] No [ ] Yes (describe, including current balances and how the accounts are held):
Column 1   Column 2

32. Do you have any Totten trust or p/o/d accounts? [ ] No [ ] Yes (describe, including the person to whom each account is payable):
Do you want to change these designations to conform to your estate plan? [ ] No [ ] Yes, as follows:
NOTE: Follow the procedures for changing the payee specified by the bank or other institution holding the account.

33. Are you the grantor of any trusts? [ ] No [ ] Yes (describe and attach a copy of each trust instrument to this inventory).

34. Do you own any collections of art, memorabilia, etc. [ ] No [ ] Yes (describe or attach inventory sheet)
    Column 1   Column 2

35. List your insurance policies and their beneficiaries.

36. List employee benefits to which you are entitled from past and present employers.

37. Who do you want to get the money in any bank accounts in your sole name at the time of your death?
    Column 1   Column 2

38. Do you have a safe deposit box [ ] No [ ] Yes (describe, including location, number, and title)
    For contents of a box in your sole name, do you want it: [ ] treated as part of your residuary estate
    [ ] contents left to a specific person, or divided among several people (explain):
    For box in joint name, indicate property that is yours rather than your co-owners, and explain any evidence useful in tracing ownership.

39. Who do you want to get the miscellaneous personal property (clothes, furniture, etc.) in your home at the time of your death?
    Column 1   Column 2

40. Do you want to leave money or property to any charities? [ ] No [ ] Yes (describe):

41. Do you want to leave money or property to anyone outside your family? [ ] No [ ] Yes (list by person, item).

42. Do you own any community property? NOTE: If you do, only half of it can be disposed of by your will—the other half goes automatically to your spouse. [ ] No [ ] Yes (describe)
    Column 1   Column 2

43. Who do you want to act as your executor? Who do you want to act as your substitute executor if the original person or organization is unable or unwilling to serve?

44. Do you own any real estate outside your home state? [ ] No [ ] Yes (describe, including location, state of title):
    Column 1   Column 2

∗∗

The information in the inventory, added to the general background information the lawyer obtains for all clients, provides the foundation for the estate plan and the will. If the potentially taxable estate falls below the unified credit amount, and the testator has never made any taxable gifts, it won't be necessary to make any elaborate arrangements to avoid federal estate tax. (However, the client should be aware that increasing prosperity is a reason to modify the estate plan and will, and the lawyer should be aware that many estates free of federal estate tax are subject to state estate or inheritance taxes.)

RECORDKEEPING

In addition to the inventory and the standard intake form used in all client files, the file of an estate planning client should contain:

- numbered and dated drafts of all wills and codicils (may be useful in establishing the testator's intentions and how they change over time)
- a summary of the testator's employee benefits
- a summary of the testator's self-provided and employer-provided insurance coverage
- copies of any separation agreements, and divorce or adoption decrees
- copies of any buy-sell agreement covering closely held business stock owned by the testator
- correspondence and notes taken during discussions with the client (may be useful in proving testamentary capacity and freedom from undue influence)
- copies of any partnership agreements (if the testator is a general or limited partner)
- copies of any disclaimers made by the testator
- copies of any antenuptial agreements between the testator and a present, past, or intended spouse.

PRACTICE TIP: It can save a lot of time to summarize the relevant provisions of each document as it is placed in the file (maybe writing or typing the summary on a sheet of colored paper for easy visibility; short summaries can be handwritten and attached to the document with adhesive note pads).

If the file gets too thick, it might be worthwhile to create three subfiles: an active file containing the latest draft of the will, the summary sheets, the inventory and intake forms; a file containing the earlier drafts; and a file containing the document copies. Then, the active file can be kept in the most accessible location, the other two placed in storage.

CARE AND CUSTODY OF THE WILL

This brings us to the question of how the executed original of the will should be stored. If the drafter will act as executor, and if he or she has adequate fireproof storage that will keep the will in good condition yet accessible, it's a good idea for the drafter to retain custody of the will.

If none of these is the case, or if the testator prefers to retain the will, the testator should be educated about the proper care of the will. For one thing, the spouse, executor, or other interested person should be informed of the will's location (and its new location, if it is moved). For another thing, the will must be preserved from dirt, inadvertant destruction during spring cleaning, fire, and water damage. The testator may have (or may, on the drafter's advice, buy) a lockable desk or filing cabinet that will meet these criteria.

A safe deposit box, which is a normal repository for important documents that must be preserved, is obviously the worst place for the will if the state in which the testator lives (and you practice) makes a policy of sealing the safe deposit boxes of decedents until a court order for their opening has been obtained.

Approximately half the states have added another option for custody of the will. A testator can deposit his or her will with the probate court during his or her lifetime; can retrieve the will to amend it or replace it with a new will; and can rely on the will being available and accessible at the time of his or her death. The states making this provision are Alaska, Arizona, Arkansas, Colorado, Iowa, Kentucky, Maine, Maryland, Massachusetts, Michigan, Minnesota, Missouri, New Mexico, North Carolina, Ohio, Oklahoma, Rhode Island, South Dakota, Tennessee, Texas, Utah, Vermont, Virginia, and Wisconsin. (Cites appear in the state chart.)

RELATED NONTESTAMENTARY DOCUMENTS

When the will is drafted, the client and drafter may want to prepare some related documents which are not, strictly speaking, testamentary.

One of the most important is what I call the "personal property letter." Twenty-two states (Alaska, Arizona, Arkansas, Colorado, Delaware, Florida, Hawaii, Idaho, Iowa, Kansas, Maine, Michigan, Minnesota, Missouri, Montana, Nebraska, Nevada, New Jersey, New Mexico, North Dakota, Utah, and Washington) allow the incorporation by reference of a letter, which does not require will formalities, but which disposes of items of personal property.

The letter is extremely useful for a young testator, who finds it difficult to project what he or she will own at the time of his or her (presumably distant) death; for a testator who owns a valued but fluctuating collection of items (for example, a collector who constantly buys and sells or trades items of the collection); and for the testator, perhaps more common in mystery fiction than in real life, who takes pleasure in altering his or her will to compensate for changes in the obsequiousness of various relatives.

LIVING WILL

Most of the states (with New York as a conspicuous abstainer) recognize the so-called Living Will, A Living Will is a request that, if the signer ever becomes comatose and terminally ill, that extraordinary means not be used to prolong the process of dying. The various state statutes differ in their details, and this is not the place to explore them thoroughly. However, there are several things to note in a cursory discussion of the Living Will. First of all, most of the state statutes either do not provide sanctions against doctors who refuse to abide by the Living Will, or provide specifically that no such sanctions will be imposed. Thus, a Living Will is generally advisory rather than compulsory. Second, the Living Will relates only to the specific and limited case of the comatose terminally ill patient, and by no means provides authorization or legal justification for euthanasia, which is illegal in all states. The Living Will does not address the case of the paralyzed patient or the patient who wants to die because of pain or incapacitation.

The Living Will certainly makes clear that the patient does not consent to the use of extraordinary means to preserve life. Your clients may want to use a "Reverse Living Will" to make it clear that they *do* want all available technological means to be used to preserve life.

The testator may want to leave a general letter of instructions to his or her survivor, perhaps incorporating the Living Will and consent to organ donation or use of his or her body for medical teaching. The letter of instruction can also contain funeral instructions (it is a poor idea to put funeral instructions in a will, which may not be opened until after the funeral) and information about the will itself, investments, savings accounts, insurance policies, and other things the family and executor should know.

Some people also want to leave a personal message, or a so-called "Ethical Will," transmitting messages of love and conveying personal values to their survivors.

REVIEW AND UPDATING

One of the most serious questions facing the will drafter is the extent to which remote contingencies must be provided for in the will itself. In a perfect world, testators would examine their estate plans and wills frequently, and would seek legal advice whenever there was a meaningful change.

In the real world, the drafter must provide for all likely and perhaps some remote contingencies: a well-drafted will should include a simultaneous death clause, an ademption clause, antilapse provisions, and a residuary clause which takes into account the possibility that a residuary beneficiary might predecease the testator.

An important part of the drafter's job is to educate the testator about the ways in which an estate plan can be influenced by changes in circumstances as well as by legal and tax changes. Given this background, the drafter has cause to hope that the testator will make another appointment when his or her personal or tax status has changed substantially.

PRACTICE TIP: If you use holiday cards to your clients as a practice-builder, you can use the theme of the holiday as a time for reflection and examination of the will and other legal devices. If you have a client newsletter, you can use projected or recently passed legislation as a springboard for a discussion about the way in which common estate plans will be affected. Furthermore, when you do other forms of legal work for a client, discuss the estate-planning implications with the client.

It is clear, for instance, that a separation or divorce is a time for reassessing the estate plan. Creation of a business entity also calls for a disposition of the entrepreneur's interest in the business, taking tax consequences into account. Even if you undertake commercial litigation for an existing business, you may find that the business's principals do not have wills at all, or have wills drafted long ago—perhaps at a time when the business owners had far fewer assets. They may also have pre-1981 wills that do not reflect the availability of the unlimited marital deduction, or pre-1982 wills that attempt to make use of the orphan's exclusion.

In short, a wise client will understand that estate planning is not a "one-shot deal," and that repeated legal consultations will be needed over his or her lifetime. From the attorney's point of view, the best outcome is for the client to return to the same firm for all estate-planning work, and for the drafting of the will to lead to repeated consultations and referral of other potential clients.

Some lawyers use wills as a "loss leader," advertising a low fee for will drafting or estate planning. This approach is counterproductive if the lawyer merely asks a few questions and prepares a "canned" will based on a statutory will form or clauses from a book (even this book) used and reused mechanically. Every client deserves a well thought out, personally designed estate plan. Formbooks (even this one) are only a tool to clarify the drafter's thinking once he or she has chosen the optimum estate plan for the client.

2

REVOCATION

Wills, unlike diamonds, are not forever. As long as the testator is alive and retains testamentary capacity, he or she has the option of altering the will as often as he or she likes (or until he or she has exhausted the patience of all available local attorneys).

For the purposes of this portfolio, we will assume that you advise all clients who want to change their wills either to execute a codicil in proper form, or to revoke the will and substitute a later will (also in proper form). So the topics of dependent relative revocation and partial intestacy caused by improper codicils or revocation will not be covered here. These topics will be covered in a later volume in the series, dealing with probate and estate administration.

There are two types of revocation: *automatic* revocation, by operation of law; and *elective* revocation, at the option of the testator. One purpose of a routine review of the will and estate plan is to make sure that automatic revocation has not occurred contrary to the wishes of the testator; and to make provisions that will conform the new will both to applicable law and the testator's wishes.

Where the desired change is fairly minor, the testator has two choices: either to revoke the will and make a new will, incorporating the changes; or to supplement the will with one or more codicils. Codicils must be executed with will formalities. ***PRACTICE TIP:*** *The real difference between a new will and a codicil is the amount of typing involved. Given the existence of computers and electronic memory typewriters, it is probably better practice to draft a new will; a thorough review of the will and estate plan is likely to turn up other changes that should be made, and that were not covered in the proposed codicils.*

What if the testator makes frequent changes in the disposition of his or her personal property (or the personal property changes frequently, as in the case of an active collection)? A codicil may be appropriate here; so may a "personal property" letter as discussed on page 97.

REVOCATION BY OPERATION OF LAW

Until the mid-nineteenth century, married women could not hold property in their separate names (although trusts could be created for their benefits); therefore, a woman's marriage would automatically revoke any will she had made while she was single. A few states adopted this provision for both sexes, or stated that marriage followed by the birth of a child would revoke a will.

Today, the majority of jurisdictions follow the rule that marriage or the birth of children may give spouses or children who are not mentioned in the will some right to challenge the will and receive a statutory share (see page 33). However, in these jurisdictions, the will itself is not revoked by the marriage or birth, and remains dispositive for all amounts that do not pass under the statute.

The majority of jurisdictions also follow the rule that a divorce or annulment revokes certain portions of a will—dispositions made to the ex-spouse, and appointments of the ex-spouse as executor and/or trustee. Property bequeathed or devised to the ex-spouse passes as if the ex-spouse had predeceased the testator. *Separation* does not revoke a will or its provisions automatically, so anyone separating from a spouse should immediately change his or her will, in case he or she dies before a divorce has been obtained. As ever, general rules must be interpreted in the light of particular state law. For instance, *Sedberry v. Johnson*, 302 SE2d 924 (N.C. App. 1983) holds that a valid separation agreement waiving all rights under the spouse's will operates as a valid waiver, even though the first spouse to die never got around to changing his will to exclude the ex-spouse. But *Matter of Foundas' Estate*, 112 Misc. 2d 973, 448 NYS2d 114 (1982), interpreting a state statute providing revocation of will provisions by documents "totally inconsistent" with the will (EPTL §3–4.3), did not find such "total inconsistency" in a separation agreement waiving the right of election and intestate share of the spouse's estate. The separation agreement did not revoke provisions of the will in favor of the testator's estranged husband. She could have required him to waive his rights under the will (not just the right of election)—or, for that matter, changed her will.

State law should also be consulted on the effect of divorce or separation on nontestamentary arrangements such as joint accounts and beneficiary designations. Under Illinois ch. 148 Para. 301, trust provisions in favor of the settler's spouse are terminated by the judicial termination of the marriage, unless the trust terms are to the contrary. But cf. *Mailey Trust,* 20 Fiduciary Reporter 597 (Pa. 1970) (divorce does not revoke provisions in a revocable trust in favor of the grantor's ex-wife) with *Miller v. First National Bank,* 637 P2d 75 (Okla. Sup. 1981) (statutory revocation of will also applies to trusts).

On beneficiary designation, see *Life Insurance Co. of North America v. Cassidy,* 35 Cal.3d 599, 200 Cal. Rptr. 28, 676 P2d 1050 (1984). In this case, a comprehensive marital settlement included a waiver by the wife of all interest in her husband's estate at death. He told his business manager to change the beneficiary designation on his life insurance policy so that the wife would no longer be the beneficiary; the change was never made. The wife didn't get the insurance proceeds, given the clear intent to exclude her, and her relinquishment of all expectancy in his estate.

A minority of jursidictions do not follow these rules: (Note: state cites that are not given here appear in the state table.)

- California: Civil Code Sec. 4532 requires all divorce decrees to include this statement: "**NOTICE:** please review your will. Unless a provision is made in the property settlement agreement, this court proceeding does not affect your will and the ability of your former spouse to take under it."

- Connecticut: a testator's marriage, or divorce, or the birth of a child will revoke any will made prior to the event and which does not make provision for the contingency. However, divorce will not revoke a will if the will made no provision for the spouse in the first place.

- Georgia: a will is revoked by marriage, divorce, or the birth of a child, unless the will provides for the contingency. However, this provision applies only to wills, not to other dispositive instruments, like designation of the testator's father as the beneficiary of his retirement benefits: *Kirksey v. Teachers Retirement System,* 302 SE2d 201 (Ga. Sup. 1983).

- Kansas adopts the conventional position on partial revocation by divorce; wills are also revoked by marriage followed by the birth or adoption of a child.

- Kentucky: marriage revokes any will made before marriage, except for a will exercising a power of appointment (over property which would *not* go to the testator's heir, personal representative, or next of kin), or a will explicitly stating that it will not be revoked by marriage.

- Louisiana: a will is revoked by the subsequent birth of a legitimate child; legitimation of an illegitimate child; or adoption of a child—unless the testator has provided for the child in the will, or unless the will states explicitly that such contingencies do not revoke the will.

- Maryland: the combination of marriage and the birth, adoption, or legitimation of a child revokes a will made before marriage; Maryland follows the majority on partial revocation by divorce.

- Massachusetts: wills are revoked by marriage, except for those wills which, on their face, were made in contemplation of marriage. Divorce provisions are conventional.

- Mississippi: wills are revoked by the birth of a child who is not mentioned in the will (unless the child dies without issue and before reaching the age of 21).

- Nevada: marriage revokes a premarriage will as to the spouse, unless the will or a contract shows an intent to *exclude* the spouse from inheriting; divorce revokes a will as to the spouse unless the separation agreement or court order is to the contrary.

- New Hampshire Sec. 551.14 reads, "The preceding section [dealing with elective revocation by destruction of an old will or execution of a replacement will] shall not control or affect any revocation of a will, implied by law, from any change in the circumstances of the testator, or his family, devisees, legatees, or estate, occurring between the time of making the will and the death of the testator." In New Hampshire, divorce does not revoke provisions made for the ex-spouse: *In the Matter of Rice*, 118 NH 528, 390 A2d 1148 (1978).

- New Jersey: the conventional provisions about the effect of absolute divorce also apply to divorce from bed and board (that is, a decree of legal separation).

- North Carolina: a will is *not* revoked by marriage, and a spouse explicitly has the right to elect against either a premarriage or postmarriage will.

- Ohio: divorce revokes provisions made in favor of an ex-spouse, unless the will provides to the contrary.

- Oregon: marriage revokes a will if the testator is survived by his or her spouse, unless the will was made in contemplation of marriage; states that it shall not be revoked by marriage; or there was an antenuptial contract. Divorce provisions are conventional.

- Rhode Island: marriage revokes wills that were not made in contemplation of marriage (but marriage does not revoke will provisions dealing with exercise of powers of appointment).

- South Carolina: marriage and/or the birth of issue of the marriage who survive the testator revoke an earlier will, unless the will was made in contemplation of marriage and provides for the spouse and/or issue; divorce revokes any provision for the ex-spouse, or appointment of the ex-spouse as a fiduciary, unless the will shows on its face that it was made in contemplation of divorce.

- South Dakota: marriage revokes a premarriage will if the spouse survives the testator, unless the will shows an intention to exclude the spouse, or unless there was provision for the spouse in the will itself or through an antenuptial contract. The birth of issue of the marriage who survive the testator revokes the will unless the will shows an intention to exclude them, or unless they were provided for in the will or by settlement.

- Washington: marriage and the spouse's surviving the testator revoke a premarriage will unless the will shows intent to exclude the spouse, or unless there is a marriage settlement or provision for the spouse in the will; divorce revokes dispositions to the ex-spouse.

- West Virginia: all wills (except wills with no provisions other than exercise of powers of appointment) are revoked by marriage, annulment, or divorce, unless the will itself makes provision for that contingency.

- Wisconsin: marriage invalidates an earlier will if the spouse survives the testator, unless the will was made in contemplation of marriage, provides for the testator's issue, or shows an intent to exclude the spouse; the will is not invalidated if there was a valid antenuptial contract.

According to a recent Tennessee case, *Re Estate of Perigen,* 653 SW2d 717 (1983), the rules about revocation of wills by changed marital circumstances are subject to exceptions. For example, in a case in which the property provisions of a divorce settlement were never implemented, and the ex-spouses cohabited after the divorce, will provisions in favor of the ex-spouse were not necessarily revoked; the case was remanded for further proceedings.

However, in Missouri (*Re Estate of Bloomer,* 620 SW2d 365 (1981), divorce revokes provisions made in favor of the ex-spouse even in a will executed before the marriage, and if the legatee was not the testator's spouse when the will was made.

Although the statutes refer to partial revocation of will provisions on divorce, in states where this is the rule, divorce may also revoke unfunded revocable pour-over trusts, where such trusts are part of an integrated estate plan: *Miller v. First National Bank and Trust,* 637 P2d 75 (Oklahoma 1981): *Clymer v. Mayo,* 393 Mass. 754, 473 NE2d 1084 (1985).

EXAMPLE: If an unmarried person comes to you to have a will drafted, the "belt and suspenders" solution is to draft a will reflecting the testator's current estate plan—and also making provision for the possibility of the testator dying survived by a spouse and/or children. But the testator must both be advised of the importance of revising the will to account for changed circumstances, and educated if the state's law (for example, South Dakota) calls for revocation of a will by marriage.

If the testator's desire to make a will is spurred by an impending marriage, the will should make clear the fact that it *is* in contemplation of marriage, and should either make provision for the spouse at least equal to the spouse's elective share or refer to an existing, valid antenuptial contract or waiver of the right of election. The will should also make provision for the possibility of the contemplated marriage not taking place.

The will of a married but childless person should cope with the possibility that children will be born—either by making a formula provision for them ("If I am survived both by a spouse and children, I direct that my estate [or the residue of my estate] be divided into equal shares, one each for my spouse and each child"), or by indicating that the children have not been forgotten, but that the surviving spouse is entrusted with their financial well-being. In states such as Louisiana, the will should indicate that the testator's intention is that the will *not* be revoked by the birth of children.

Given the prevalence of divorce, married testators who name their spouses as executors must give thought to the designation of successor executor—in the not-too-uncommon case that the appointment of the ex-spouse as executor is revoked.

ELECTIVE REVOCATION

All the states provide two alternative forms of elective revocation: destruction of a will *animo revocandi* (with intent to revoke), and execution of a subsequent will. It is a good idea to remind clients that destruction of a will (defacing, cutting, tearing, burning) can be used to effect complete revocation of a will, but not partial revocation (see NY EPTL § 3–4.1; *Estate of Haurin,* 43 Colo. App. 279, 605 P2d 65 (1979) for example. Partial revocation requires a codicil, or a new will.)

The introductory language to virtually every will recites that the document is the testator's last will, and that he or she revokes all earlier wills and codicils. It is also common for the testator to recite that he or she is of sound mind, although, of course, testamentary capacity cannot be created by this recitation. (The same level of testamentary capacity is required for valid *revocation* of a will as for creation of one.)

If the state permits incorporation by reference, it may be possible to refer to an earlier will or codicil, and to republish them as part of the new will, but it seems easier and safer to simply revoke the earlier testamentary instruments, and adopt any of the earlier language that seems useful as part of a new will.

It *is* possible to use a codicil to revoke a will, but normally a codicil republishes the earlier will except for the changes made by the codicil. (See the sample codicil forms.)

Probate courts prefer testacy to intestacy, and will make all reasonable efforts to find a probateable will, for example, *In re Thompson's Estate,* 214 Neb. 899, 336 NW2d 590 (1983), construing a statute permitting revocation either by voluntary destruction or by a properly executed later will. The testator's son said that he had seen a later, signed will revoking the will submitted for probate. However, he could not produce the alleged later will. The court found that there was no evidence of proper execution of the alleged second will, hence the earlier will would not be revoked because the effect would be to produce intestacy.

3

WILL FORMALITIES

The formalities required of a will are minimal; to be admissible to probate, a will need only be written on something that can be brought into court and signed by the testator and attested by witnesses in the proper form.

A tape recording, it has been held, does not constitute a valid will—even a holographic one—because it is not written at all, much less written in the testator's handwriting: *Estate of Reed*, 672 P.2d 829 (Wyoming 1983). However, the tape recording *may* be admissible, for example to show the testator's intent to make inter vivos gifts: *In re Roth's Estate*, 15 Oh. Op.2d 234, 170 NE2d 313 (1960).

A signed carbon copy can be admitted to probate as a valid will, given testimony that it is what the testator signed. In such a case, the carbon copy is the "original" of the will: *Backlund Will*, 30 Fiduciary Reporter 141 (Pa. 1980). Similarly, an executed photocopy can be admitted to probate (*Estate of Lewis*, NYLJ 11/1/79 p. 11), but it is better to make sure that the testator and witnesses sign the ribbon copy. ***PRACTICE TIP:*** *offering an executed photocopy for probate tends to create the inference that multiple originals were executed (all of which must be produced for probate), or that the other copies were destroyed with revocatory intent. It is also easy to tamper with photocopies.*

Choice of Law: The validity of the execution of a will is determined according to the law of the state in which it is executed, but the will must be proved according to the law of the forum in which it is admitted for probate: *Will of Keane,* 417 NYS2d 28, 99 Misc. 2d 714 (Surrogates' Court 1979); however, the validity of a devise of real property depends on the law of the situs of the property. If the will covers realty in more than one state, the devises are to be interpreted as if there were several wills, made in the appropriate states: *In re Swanson's Estate,* 397 So2d 465 (Fla. App. 1981). Fortunately, at least one state has a presumption that a will prepared by an attorney is in proper form: *Matter of Hughson,* 97 Misc. 2d 427, 411 NYS2d 839 (1978). That this presumption is rebuttable can be seen by the cases discussed under "Malpractice Traps."

State statutes demand that wills be written and signed, and that they be witnessed. As we will see in the next chapter, there are some substantive limitations on a testator's freedom to dispose of his or her property as he or she sees fit: a married testator must consider the effect of the spouse's right of election, and pretermitted (unmentioned) spouses and children may have a right of forced heirship. However, state statutes do not impose procedural requirements on the dispositive provisions of a will: any form of language or organization may be used. The will drafter's task is to be clear, and to dispose of all disposable property, but there are no mandatory structures to follow, and no "code words" need to be used if the drafter prefers to omit them. It is not required that the pages of the will be typed at the same time, or on the same kind of paper, provided that the will is complete when it is offered to the testator for signing: *Succession of Norton,* 451 So2d 1203 (La. 1984).

SIGNATURE

A formal will must be signed by the testator (or by a person acting for him or her in the case of a physical inability to sign). In most states, the testator signs only once, at the end of the will. However, Louisiana testators must sign each page of the will, in the presence of the witnesses and of a notary.

Like any other seemingly obvious term, the phrase "end of the will" can be the subject of legal controversy. The New York statute (EPTL §3-2.1) states that if a will presented for probate contains material (other than the attestation clause, of course) after the testator's signature, the will shall not be invalidated by the presence of the additional material. However, the additional material will not be given effect unless the will is incomprehensible without it. ***PRACTICE TIP:*** *Thus, the drafter must be careful to avoid "afterthoughts," and to make sure that the pages are collated in the correct order.*

As an example of the New York statute, and of principles of construction applicable in other states, consider *Matter of Hall,* 118 Misc. 2d 1052, 462 NYS2d 154 (Surr. 1983) and *Will of Mergenthaler,* 123 Misc. 2d 809, 474 NYS2d 253 (Surr. 1984). *Hall* involved the introduction for probate of a will with a missing page; pages numbered 1, 2, 3, and 5 were offered. As it turned out, the client had signed the will in that condition; the four pages set out a complete dispositive scheme and made the necessary appointment of fiduciaries, without reference to page 4 (which dealt with legatees under a disability—as it turned out, none of the legatees was under a disability when the will was offered for probate—and included boilerplate clauses dealing with fiduciary powers). The will was admitted to probate, but the loose copy of page 4 offered to the court was not admitted to probate, because it had not been part of the instrument actually signed by the testator.

The *Mergenthaler* case involved a will whose pages were stapled in the wrong order. The will, as signed, contained pages 1, 2, an unnumbered page containing the signatures of the testator and witnesses, and page 3 containing the residuary clause and the clause defining the powers of the executor. The court admitted pages 1, 2, and the unnumbered page to probate, because they formed a complete and consistent scheme of disposition, but refused to give effect to the material on page 3. The omission of page 3 did not subvert the testator's intentions, because the residue of the estate passed under the rules of intestate succession. The rules of intestate succession benefited the testator's nephew, who was the residuary legatee specified on page 3. In the Arkansas case of *Scritchfield v. Loyd,* the will was permitted to be probated with the testator's signature in the attestation clause because he thought it belonged there, and because he signed with testamentary intent.

However, the "will" in the case of *Matter of Zaharis' Estate,* 91 AD2d 737, 457 NYS2d 995 (1982), *aff'd* 463 NYS2d 195, was not admitted to probate. The will was a 3 × 5 card with writing on both sides. The testator's signature appeared in the right margin on the front of the card; the witnesses signed in the lower right of the back of the card. The dispositive provisions ended three and one-half lines from the bottom of the back of the card, and there was room to sign there. That was the "end" of the will, and the only proper place for a signature of a will admissible to probate.

Similarly, *Matter of Agar,* NYLJ 7/1/82 p. 5, holds that the alleged will should not have been probated. The "will" was two hand-written sheets, not attached to one another, with no attestation clause. The testator's signature appeared on the second page, followed by the signatures, names, and addresses of two witnesses. There was, however, no proof that the alleged will had consisted of only two pages, nor that the testator signed in the witness' presence or acknowledged his signature before them.

The Michigan Court of Appeals remanded the case of *Matter of Dodson's Estate,* 119 Mich. App. 427, 326 NW2d 532 (1982), for further proceedings. The will submitted for probate was on a two-page will form, with no clear indication of whether or not the pages were joined. The testator signed only once, on the first page. The signature was made with testamentary intent, but the testator neither signed at the end of the form nor in the space provided for signature. The witnesses signed only once, on the second page. The remand permitted the proponents to introduce extrinsic evidence that the two pages were presented to the witnesses in a way that indicated that they were a single document.

ATTESTATION

A formal will requires not merely the testator's signature, but attestation by witnesses. Although state statutes vary in the technical details (see the cites in the state chart), a drafter who follows this procedure should produce a document admissible for probate in any state:

- Testator assembles three credible adult witnesses, none of whom receives anything under the will, and none of whom is married to a legatee.
- In the presence of these witnesses, the testator informs them that the document is his or her will.
- The testator then signs the will at its end.
- All the witnesses sign the will in the testator's presence and in the presence of the other witnesses, in an attestation clause after the testator's signature and identified as such.
- All the witnesses then sign a self-proving affidavit, still in the testator's presence and in the presence of the other witnesses.

In most states, having three witnesses is a "belt and suspenders" strategy, because only two witnesses are required; however, South Carolina and Vermont require three.

Under normal circumstances, the will-signing ceremony should be a fairly private one: it is certainly proper for the drafter to be present, but it looks bad for a beneficiary to be present during the execution of the will, or the discussions leading up to the drafting of the will (*Re Davis' Estate*, 438 So.2d 543 (Fla. App. 1983); *Webster v. Kennebrew*, 443 So.2d 850 (Miss. 1983). *Kennebrew* also states that the subscribing witnesses should be acquainted with the testator, which militates against the common practice of using employees of the drafter's law firm (who are most unlikely to be legatees) as witnesses.

State laws vary as to whether the witnesses must see the testator sign, or whether they may sign after he or she does if he or she acknowledges that the signature is his or hers. See, for example, *O'Neal v. Jennings*, 53 Md. App. 631, 455 A.2d 66 (1983); *In re Estate of Flicker*, 215 Neb. 495, 339 NW2d 914 (1983); *Davis v. Davis*, 471 A.2d 1008 (D.C. 1984).

New York has an unusual procedure (EPTL Sec. 3-2.1): the witnesses may sign within thirty days of the testator's signature, and there is a rebuttable presumption that the thirty-day requirement has been met.

In Nebraska, the witnesses may also sign after the will has been signed; the *Flicker* case, previously cited, adds the common-sense proviso that the testator must still be alive when his or her will is signed; as the court said, permitting witnesses to sign a document after its maker is dead would limit the effectiveness of the attestation requirement to preclude fraud and mistake. Similarly, see *Estate of Padilla,* 97 NM 508, 641 P2d 539 (1982), in which presumption of due execution in a will signed by the testator and two witnesses was found, despite the witness's testimony that they signed at different times, and did not observe the testator's or the other witness's signature.

Many states require "publication"; that is, the testator must inform the witnesses that the document is his or her will. See, *Matter of Kelly's Estate,* 99 NM 482, 660 P.2d 124 (1983), for example. Publication is required, but no particular form is mandated; publication can be done by conduct, and the statement that the document is the testator's will can be made by someone else, and affirmed by the testator. In other states, particularly states adopting the Uniform Probate Code, publication is not required (for example, in North Dakota; see *Matter of Estate of Polda,* 349 NW2d 11 (ND 1984).

Generally, the witnesses are witnessing only a signature; and, either by statute or by case law, many states provide that no particular form of attestation clause is required. See Pennsylvania Title 20 Sec. 2502; Rhode Island Sec. 33-5-5; Virginia Sec. 64.1-49; West Virginia Sec. 41-1-3; *In re Cutsinger,* 445 P.2d 778 (Oklahoma 1968); *Succession of Augustus,* 441 So.2d 730 (Louisiana 1983—but the will being construed came from the District of Columbia); and *Matter of Kelly's Estate,* 99 NM 482, 660 P.2d 124 (1983) as examples. Texas goes a step further, and permits witnesses to sign anywhere in the will, as long as they sign with intent to act as witnesses. See *Mossler v. Johnson,* 565 SW2d 952 (Texas 1978) for example. Georgia's *Newton v. Palmour,* 266 SE2d 208 (1980), addresses the other end of the question, whether the testator must observe the witnesses signing the will for it to be valid. The holding is that this is not literally required, so long as the testator *could* have seen the witnesses without changing position.

Louisiana handles this in a different manner. The case of *Succession of Brown,* 458 So.2d 140 (Louisiana 1984) requires that the testator sign each page of the will, and sign at the end of the will, all in the presence of a notary and at least two competent witnesses; the testator must declare that the instrument is his or her will; and the notary and the witnesses (in the presence of the testator and each other) must sign either the attestation clause provided by statute, or one that is very similar. An attestation clause that fails to recite that the notary and witnesses signed the will on the relevant date, in the presence of the testators and the others, is fatally defective and will preclude probate of the will.

A few state statutes (California, New York, South Dakota) specify that the witnesses should give their addresses as part of the attestation clause; but they also specify that the will cannot be invalidated by the absence of these addresses.

Usually, the witnesses sign merely to indicate that they have witnessed a signature. A minority of the states do require the witnesses to indicate that they believe the testator to have testamentary capacity and/or to be free of undue influence. See, for example, Indiana Sec. 29-1-5-3 (self-proving affidavit); New Jersey Sec. 3B:3-4 (testator declares that he or she is of sound mind and the will is signed willingly, without duress or undue influence; the witnesses state that, to the best of their knowledge, this declaration is correct); *In re Camin's Estate*, 212 Neb. 490, 323 NW2d 827 (1982) (witness must believe, "to the best of his knowledge," that the testator is of sound mind, but has no obligation to inquire; failure to observe will not invalidate the will. Lack of personal knowledge of the testator's mental condition goes to the weight of the witness's testimony, not its admissibility.) Of course, if there is a will contest, the witnesses in the other states will be required to testify about the testator's mental condition and the absence or presence of undue influence.

Interested Witnesses A witness who is also a legatee has a certain degree of motivation to uphold the will, even if he or she has some reservations about the testator's testamentary capacity or other element of validity of the will or propriety of its execution. Therefore, the major function of having wills witnessed—to permit an examination of the circumstances surrounding the execution of the will, at a time after the main actor has become entirely unavailable for questioning—is impaired.

But a witness who is also a distributee (heir under a scheme of intestacy) has a countervailing motivation, to upset the will so that he or she can take his or her intestate share.

Balancing these two temptations, all the states provide that no will is invalid simply because it is attested by one or more interested witnesses. (In fact, in Virginia an interested witness is completely competent to testify in a will contest: §64.1-51.)

The general rule is that an interested witness who is not a distributee (a friend or lover of the testator's; a faithful employee singled out for a legacy) may not take under the will unless there are other, disinterested witnesses (usually two—that is, if the interested witness's attestation is superfluous). Many states provide that an interested witness who is a distributee may take his or her intestate share in any event, but may not take more than the intestate share unless there is an adequate complement of disinterested witnesses. Some states also characterize a witness as interested if his or her spouse is a legatee. See *In re Johnson's Estate*, 359 So.2d 425 (Fla. 1978); *Rogers v. Helmes*, 69 Oh. St.2d 323, 432 NE2d 186 (1982); *Dorfman v. Allen*, 386 Mass. 121,434 NE2d 1012 (1982).

PRACTICE TIP: In short, having a will witnessed by a legatee is not fatal to the will, and may not even be fatal to the legatee's expectations under the will; however, it is much better practice for the drafter to locate witnesses who are not takers under the will.

SELF-PROOF

Most of the states permit the use of a self-proving affidavit. (The states are Alabama, Alaska, Arizona, Arkansas, Colorado, Connecticut, Delaware, Florida, Georgia, Hawaii, Idaho, Indiana, Iowa, Kansas, Kentucky, Maine, Minnesota, Missouri, Montana, Nebraska, Nevada, New Hampshire, New Jersey, New Mexico,

North Carolina, North Dakota, Oklahoma, Pennsylvania, Rhode Island, South Carolina, South Dakota, Texas, Utah, Virginia, Washington, West Virginia, and Wyoming; cites are in the state table.) In fact, all valid New Hampshire post-1984 wills *must* be self-proved.

A self-proving affidavit streamlines the probate process by making it unnecessary to call the witnesses (who may be difficult to find by the time the will is probated, or who may themselves be dead or incompetent) to testify to the due execution of the will. Thus, a self-proving affidavit (a sample, taken from Uniform Probate Code 2-504, is reproduced on page 31) allows the witnesses to state, under oath, that they believe the testator to be of full age and sound mind; that the document signed is his or her will; and that the signature on the document is that of the testator—more or less what they would testify to if they were called as part of a will contest.

The effect of the affidavit is to preclude a challenge to the "due execution" of the will—that is, it establishes that the will formalities were complied with—but does not prevent a challenge based on lack of testamentary capacity or on the presence of undue influence. (*In re Rosborough's Estate,* 542 SW2d 685 (Tex. Civ. App. 1976); *In re Flider's Estate,* 213 Neb. 153, 328 NW2d 197 (1982)).

In some states, a will can be probated if the witnesses sign the self-proving affidavit but fail to sign the will itself (*In re Estate of Cutsinger,* 445 P.2d 778 (Oklahoma 1968); *In re Estate of Charry,* 359 So.2d 544 (Florida 1978); *Matter of Estate of Petty,* 227 Kan. 697, 608 P.2d 987 (1980)). An Illinois case, *Matter of Estate of Cornelius,* 80 Ill. Dec. 687, 465 NE2d 1033 (1984), permitted an ordinary attestation clause to act as a self-proving affidavit, because the attestation clause recited that the witnesses, believing that the testator was of sound mind and memory, signed the document that they believed to be the testator's last will, in the testator's presence and the presence of the other witnesses. The *Cornelius* court's holding was that this recitation replaced the testimony the witnesses would have offered.

However, the weight of authority is that a will cannot be offered for probate if the self-proving affidavit is signed but the witnesses failed to sign the will itself: *Douthit v. McLeroy,* 539 SW2d 351 (Texas 1976); *Matter of Sample's Estate,* 175 Mont. 93, 572 P.2d 1232 (1977); *Matter of McDougal's Estate,* 552 SW2d 587 (Tex. Civ. App. 1977); *Matter of Mackaben's Estate,* 126 Ariz. 599, 617 P.2d 765 (1980); *Rodgers v. King's Estate,* 614 SW2d 896 (Tex. Civ. App. 1981); *Wich v. Fleming,* 652 SW2d 353 (Texas 1983). Under this theory, the affidavit is an attachment to the will, but not part of the will itself. Therefore, if the witnesses sign only the affidavit, the will itself is fatally defective and cannot be probated.

PRACTICE TIPS: *What can the lawyer do to ensure a trouble-free creation of a will? As the cases discussed above show, innovation can lead to trouble; so can old-fashioned sloppiness. 1) The first step is to proofread the will carefully before it is submitted to the client for signature. That way, the need for additions and corrections (potential sources of controversy) is minimized or eliminated. Especially if you have access to word-processing, you can offer the client a perfect draft—and one that is printed out on only one side of the page, on normal 8-1/2 x 11 inch paper.*

2) Of course, you must make sure that the pages are correctly numbered and presented in the correct order. It is all too easy for the person preparing the document to number page 4 as page 5, or to number two different pages as page 3, or simply to omit a page.

3) Finally, make sure that there is adequate space for the testator's signature, wherever required. If your state recognizes the self-proving affidavit, and you choose to use it, make sure that the testator and witnesses sign both the will itself and the affidavit. Otherwise, make sure that the will is signed "at the end."

4) Try to exclude extraneous people from the attestation ceremony; make sure that interested witnesses are not used; and remember that "publication" may be absolutely required in your state, and certainly cannot hurt in other states. Before the signing ceremony, make sure that any addresses required by your state are added at the appropriate parts of the will.

Self-Proving Affidavit

I, _____, the testator, sign my name to this instrument this _____ day of _____, 19 ____, and being first duly sworn, do hereby declare to the undersigned authority that I sign and execute this instrument as my last will and that I sign it willingly (or willingly direct another to sign for me), that I execute it as my free and voluntary act for the purposes therein expressed, and that I am eighteen years of age or older, of sound mind, and under no constraint or undue influence.

_____
Testator

We, _____, _____, the witnesses, sign our names to this instrument, being first duly sworn, and do hereby declare to the undersigned authority that the testator signs and executes this instrument as his last will and that he signs it willingly (or willingly directs another to sign for him), and that each of us, in the presence and hearing of the testator, hereby signs this will as witness to the testator's signing, and that to the best of our knowledge the testator is eighteen years of age or older, of sound mind, and under no constraint or undue influence.

_____
Witness

_____
Witness

The State of _____
County of _____
    Subscribed, sworn to the acknowledged before me
by _____, the testator, and subscribed and sworn to before
me by _____, and _____, witnesses, this _____ day of
_____.

(Seal)

               (Signed) _____

              _____
              (Official capacity of officer)

    An attested will may at any time subsequent to its execution be made
self-proved by the acknowledgment thereof by the testator and the
affidavits of the witnesses, each made before an officer authorized to
administer oaths under the laws of the state where the acknowledgement
occurs and evidenced by the officer's certificate, under the official seal,
attached or annexed to the will in substantially the following form:

The State of _____
County of _____
    We, _____, _____, and _____,
the testator and the witnesses, respectively, whose names are signed to
the attached or foregoing instrument, being first duly sworn, do hereby
declare to the undersigned authority that the testator signed and executed
the instrument as his last will and that he had signed willingly (or willingly
directed another to sign for him), and that he executed it as his free and
voluntary act for the purposes therein expressed, and that each of the
witnesses, in the presence and hearing of the testator, signed the will as
witness and that to the best of his knowledge the testator was at that time
eighteen years of age or older, of sound mind and under no constraint or
undue influence.

              _____
                          Testator

              _____
                          Witness

              _____
                          Witness

    Subscribed, sworn to and acknowledged before me
by _____, the testator, and subscribed and sworn to before
me by _____, and _____, witnesses, this
_____ day of _____.
(Seal)

               (Signed) _____

              _____
             (Official capacity of officer)

CODICILS

As discussed earlier, the codicil may become an anachronism: given electronic typewriters and word processors, it is just as easy to draft a full new will. Furthermore, the new will gives the testator the opportunity to reexamine the estate plan in light of changes in circumstances and tax law.

However, until that time, drafters must be concerned about the form of codicils, and their effect. A codicil must be executed with will formalities. It must be clear whether the codicil revokes or merely supplements the provisions of an existing will that is intended to continue in force. The codicil must also make it clear whether it is intended to revoke earlier *codicils,* if any were made.

The interesting case of *Unitarian Universalist Service of Boston v. Lebrecht,* 670 SW2d 402 (Tex. 1984), which turns on the interpretation of a semicolon (whether four charities were each intended to take 25 percent of a bequest, or whether half the bequest went to one charity, the other half to the remaining three), holds that a will and codicil must be construed together as one—and as if they had been executed on the date of the codicil. (Extrinsic evidence was allowed to clarify the testator's intent.)

Under *Gilbert. v. Gilbert,* 652 SW2d 663 (Ky. App. 1983), a testator can have more than one effective will at a given time, each covering part of the estate, but the later documents operate as codicils.

Therefore, you must examine codicils just as carefully for latent ambiguity as you would a full-scale will, and be very careful about punctuation.

SUMMARY

Even outside the states that disqualify a will because only the self-proving affidavit is signed, it is simple enough for the drafter to prevent controversy by making sure that the witnesses sign the will itself. In fact, there are few technical problems involved in satisfying state statutes dealing with will formalities. There are more difficult technical problems in the subject of the next chapter—dealing with limitations on the testator's freedom to select a dispositive scheme (right of election, pretermission, and disinheritance) and the following chapter (special drafting problems such as testamentary capacity, remote contingencies, and dispositions of personal property).

4

LIMITS ON TESTAMENTARY FREEDOM

The general rule is that the testator may dispose of his or her property entirely as he or she wishes. However, there are exceptions to the rule. Certain items that the testator thinks of as "his" or "her" property may be jointly owned, and thus pass outside the will; testators in community property states are permitted to control only half the community property by will.

Furthermore, the wills of married testators generally are subject to the spouse's *right of election*. That is, a spouse who receives less than the statutory elective share under the will may challenge the will and receive the elective share in lieu of the smaller, testamentary provision; the other provisions of the will must then be adjusted to compensate. The exceptions to this exception to the general rule: wills of testators who are parties to valid antenuptial agreements, and wills of testators who have received valid disclaimers of the right of election.

If the testator has children, the children will be protected by the laws of most states, which provide that "pretermitted heirs"—children or other natural heirs who are not mentioned in the will—are presumed to be omitted by mistake, and therefore are entitled to a statutory share of the estate. This presumption can be overcome if the children are mentioned in the will (not necessarily bequeathed or devised any property) or if the will makes provision for afterborn children.

Apart from the spouse's elective share, the testator is generally free to disinherit his or her natural heirs, provided that the appropriate formalities are observed.

Some testators, anxious to preserve their testamentary schemes, use the *in terrorem* clause—a clause disinheriting anyone mentioned in the will who initiates or participates in a will contest. Although the *in terrorem* clause is valid and enforceable in most states, some states impose a statutory or case-law limitation, invalidating the clause wherever the will contestants have probable cause for their challenge to the will.

SPOUSE'S ELECTIVE SHARE

Nearly all the common-law (noncommunity property) jurisdictions permit spouses to elect against the will; the exceptions are Georgia, (but a will disinheriting spouse or children will receive "close scrutiny"—§53-2-9) Missouri, and Rhode Island. The elective share is not really necessary in community property states, because the surviving spouse inherits half the community property outside the will. (Cites for elective-share statutes are given in the state table.)

The usual formulation is that the spouse may elect against the will and receive the proportion of the deceased spouse's estate that he or she would have received if the testator had died intestate rather than with a will providing less than the elective share for the spouse. The will itself is not the only thing to be considered; provision for the spouse outside the will (insurance policies or transfer of separate property or the testator's share of joint property to the spouse, for example) must be taken into account in determining the adequacy of the will provision, and thus the right of election. However, the Florida formulation is that the elective share is 30 percent of the fair market value of the gross estate, less valid claims against the estate and mortgages, liens, and security interests on the estate.

Also see the discussion of revocation by operation of law on pages 18-22. In effect, the spouse has an automatic right of election if the will is revoked by marriage and survival of the spouse. However, in a state with a right of election, the basic testamentary scheme remains in force after the spouse has exercised the right of election (although, of course, the other legacies must be adjusted to provide the spouse's elective share). In a state providing for revocation of the will, the would-be testator is considered to have died intestate, and the state's intestate inheritance scheme is applied.

A number of states (Alabama, Alaska, Arizona, California, Colorado, Connecticut, Delaware, Florida, Idaho, Maine, Michigan, Mississippi, Missouri, Montana, Nebraska, New Mexico, North Dakota, Pennsylvania, Utah, Virginia, Washington) make provision for the pretermitted spouse—that is, they permit a spouse who is not mentioned in the will to take an intestate share of the estate. This situation is slightly different from that of the spouse who is mentioned in the will, but who is supposed to inherit less than his or her statutory elective share.

The Florida election and pretermitted-spouse statutes have been construed several times by the courts. For example, the case of *Estate of Ganier v. Estate of Ganier*, 418 So.2d 256 (Fla. 1982) involves a will executed before the testator's marriage, and not in contemplation of marriage; it provided for his eventual spouse, describing her as a "friend." The court's holding is that Mrs. Ganier was entitled to elect against the will, because the will did not provide for her in her role of spouse. Under this holding, a will escapes the pretermitted-spouse statute only if it provides for the spouse *and* is either executed after the marriage or in contemplation of marriage. *Solomon v. Dunlap*, 372 So.2d 218 (Fla. App. 1979) makes it clear that the pretermitted spouse's share is taken from the net value of the estate, not the gross estate; if the legislature's intent had been to permit the pretermitted spouse to inherit free of taxes, debts, and administrative costs the statute would have so provided.

The 1982 North Dakota case of *Matter of Knudsen's Estate*, 322 NW2d 454, involves a will providing for "my wife Lisa," but the testator was married to another woman, Susan, when he died. The court permitted Susan Knudsen to elect against the will although she received more than the statutory one-third of the augmented estate, once non-will transfers were taken into account. Summary judgment was not granted, because there was evidence that the testator was worried about his failure to provide adequately for Susan.

EXAMPLE: Harold Lifton makes a will in 1984, after his 1981 marriage to Alice Carraway Lifton; they have no children. (Thus, the will is not revoked by his marriage, because it is subsequent to the marriage; nor can the marriage be revoked by the birth of children, because they have none.) The will does not mention Alice, leaving all his property to his brother, two of his nieces, and the American Cancer Society.

If the Liftons live in one of the states mentioned above as having a pretermitted-spouse statute, Alice will be entitled to an intestate share of the estate. If they live in one of the other states, she may be entitled to elect against the will—*if* she has never validly executed a waiver of this right; and if the non-testamentary provision for her (property she inherits as surviving joint tenant or tenant by the entireties) is not sufficient under the state's law.

However, Alice may have adequate funds of her own, and may prefer not to disturb her husband's testamentary scheme; so she might decide not to exercise her right or election or right as a pretermitted spouse.

ANTENUPTIAL AGREEMENTS

It is possible for a prospective spouse to waive all interest in the future spouse's estate, or to waive the right of election; however, such a waiver must be knowing, intelligent, and based on full disclosure of the assets and interests being waived.

Although some states have case law saying that antenuptial contracts are favored by the law and others have case laws saying that they are disfavored, the bottom line is that judges will tend to find a way to invalidate antenuptial agreements if they believe that the spouse seeking to invalidate the agreement got a raw deal. *PRACTICE TIP: Therefore, drafters of antenuptial agreements must be sure to make it clear that the waiving spouse was fully informed of his or her rights and the extent of the other spouse's property; it would be a good idea for a lawyer representing a prospective spouse seeking an antenuptial agreement to suggest that the other spouse be represented by counsel. The agreement itself should recite either that the agreement is the product of negotiation between attorneys for both spouses-to-be, or that the waiving spouse has been advised of his or her right to counsel and has agreed to proceed without an attorney.*

For instance, the case of *Estate of Banker*, 416 Mich. 681, 331 NW2d 193 (1983) holds that the plaintiff, who sought to invalidate an antenuptial contract, met her burden of proof as to nondisclosure. She had waived all right of inheritance or election; her husband was secretive about his financial affairs and their marital standard of living did not reflect his true means; and she had not been represented by counsel. Therefore, there was a presumption of *nondisclosure* under the circumstances, and the presumption was not overcome. A grossly disproportionate provision for the spouse may be held to create a presumption of nondisclosure, or even deliberate concealment: see *Faver v. Faver*, 266 Ark. 262 (1979), for example.

For post-1979 agreements (the provisions are not retroactive), *Rosenberg v. Lipnick*, 383 NE2d 385 (Mass. Sup. Jud. Ct. 1979) defines the requisites as follows:

- fair and reasonable provision, determined as of the execution of the agreement, for the contesting party
- full disclosure of assets, unless the contestant had, or should have had, independent knowledge
- waiver by the contestant of rights in these assets

Under *Rosenberg*, the parties' respective ages, business acumen, net worth, and prior family ties are also factors to be considered.

Roberts v. Estate of Roberts, 664 SW2d 634 (Missouri 1984), says that it is a good idea (although not strictly necessary) to list all of each fiancé's property in an antenuptial contract; even absent complete itemization, evidence can be admitted in a will contest to show that each knew the extent of the other's property.

PRACTICE TIP: Counsel should be very careful to specify the property involved in the waiver, or, more to the point, to specify it correctly. Consider Topper v. Stewart, 449 So.2d 373 (Florida 1984), which held that an antenuptial contract dealing only with real property did not constitute a waiver of the right of election against the testator's personal property owned before the marriage, or traceable proceeds of that personal property arising from postmarriage transactions.

The drafter should also make sure that any conditions specified in the antenuptial agreement are met. See *In re Estate of Harrison,* 456 Pa. 356, 319 A2d 5 (1974). The waiving spouse was permitted to elect against the will, because the antenuptial contract said that the waiver was in return for the bequest of a specified amount, and the will contained no such bequest. Similarly, an antenuptial contract premised on specified will provisions is unenforceable if the other spouse dies intestate. See *Estate of Schwartz,* 94 Misc. 2d 1024, 405 NYS2d 1024 (1978), *aff'd* 413 NYS2d 1023.

PRETERMITTED CHILD

Frequently, testators make wills many years before their deaths. Almost as frequently, they neglect to update their wills to account for changed circumstances. Thus, an unmarried testator may marry and become a parent. If the will was made in contemplation of marriage, it will almost certainly include provision for the spouse-to-be (if only to refer to an antenuptial agreement excluding the future spouse from inheriting) and is likely to make provision for any children the couple plan to have. But if the will is drafted out of a concern with tidiness and proper financial planning, it may refer only to events as of the time of the drafting of the will, not those that may occur in the future. If such a testator marries later, he or she may die without making testamentary provision for children.

In most cases, the testator did not wish to disinherit his or her children; the omission was accidental, based on poor estate planning. Therefore, to protect the children and carry out the presumed wishes of the parent, nearly all the states have "pretermitted heir" statutes. (The exceptions are Georgia, Hawaii, Kansas, New Jersey, and Wyoming; cites for the other statutes are found in the statute table.)

Under a typical pretermitted heir statute, if the will does not make provision for the testator's children (either by making financial provisions or by mentioning them and making it clear that they are not to inherit), the omitted children are entitled to an intestate share of the estate, and the explicit legacies will be adjusted to compensate for the share of the omitted children. Some statutes limit the protection of pretermitted children to those born or adopted after the drafting of the will, on the theory that the testator could hardly have been unaware of the existence of children already born when the will was drafted, and therefore the omission will be presumed intentional rather than unintentional. But Nevada takes the opposite tack: the omission of a child or the issue of a deceased child is presumed *intentional*, but the probate court can order an intestate share for the child or grandchild if the omission can be proved to be unintentional.

EXAMPLE: In 1986, Linda Grady is 24, unmarried, and has no matrimonial plans. However, one of the benefits offered by her employer is a prepaid legal services plan that offers drafting of a simple will. Figuring that the employer has paid for the plan (in effect decreasing the amount of money available for her salary), Linda takes advantage of this service, and a routine "boiler plate" will, which does not refer to the possibilities of marriage or children, is drafted and signed. Ms. Gray forgets all about it, and never bothers to have another will drafted.

In 1989, Linda marries David Monroney; their children, David Jr. and Anita, are born in 1991 and 1994 respectively. In 1995, Linda Gray Monroney is killed in an airplane accident during a business trip. Her husband finds the 1986 will in a box of miscellaneous papers. David Jr. and Anita are pretermitted children.

As discussed earlier, some statutes in effect protect the pretermitted child by invalidating a will made before the birth of the child (or invalidate the will if the unmentioned child survives the parent-testator).

If one of the testator's children predeceases the testator, the testator's children's children may be entitled to treatment as pretermitted heirs. In the case of *Smith v. Crook*, 160 Cal. App. 3d 245, 206 Cal. Rptr. 524 (1984), the residuary clause benefited the testator's three surviving children, and mentioned the testator's predeceased child, June, but not her children. The drafter of the will testified that the testator had wanted to leave "nothing to June or her heirs," but they were entitled to take as pretermitted heirs, because the will's expression of intent, not extrinsic evidence, is controlling.

Thus, for instance, in *Re Estate of Bouchat*, 37 Wash. App. 304, 679 P2d 426 (1984), the testator, estranged from his children, wrote into the will "I have no children," and "Lilly and Frank (whom he described as step-children) get nothing." There was a clear intent to exclude them, so they were not within the ambit of the pretermitted heir statute. But in *Estate of Padilla*, 97 NM 508, 641 P2d 539 (NM 1982), the testator signed a preprinted will form including a clause, "I declare that I have no children whom I have omitted to name or provide for herein." His acknowledged illegitimate son was permitted to take as a pretermitted child; the court's holding was that there must be an affirmative intention not to provide for children, not just a negative one (as failing to strike out the clause).

Under *Estate of Powers*, 454 NE2d 384 (Ill. App. 1983), a testator's afterborn children were not treated as pretermitted heirs, because he expressly disinherited the two children who were alive when the will was executed; the court's holding was that there was a consistent testamentary plan of excluding all children (whether or not born before execution of the will) from inheritance.

When the testator does explicitly disinherit his or her children, the reason given need not be a satisfactory one—for example, a provision disinheriting the testator's children by his second marriage, because they were "raised by their mother after 1 year of age" was held not void as against public policy: *Brown v. Drake*, 275 SC 299, 270 SE2d 130 (1980).

Pretermitted heir statutes referring to wills omitting reference to the testator's children do not give rise to rights in revocable trusts created by the testator; *Estate of Mayo*, 117 Wisc.2d 154, 342 NW2d 785 (1984).

IN TERROREM (NO CONTEST) CLAUSES

In general, an *in terrorem* clause (one that revokes a bequest if the recipient institutes or participates in a will contest) is valid and enforceable. However, several state statutes alter this general rule. In Georgia, for example, an *in terrorem* clause is void unless there is a gift over.

Nine states (Alaska, Hawaii, Idaho, Maryland, Michigan, Montana, Nebraska, New Jersey, and North Dakota) provide that an *in terrorem* clause is void if there is reasonable cause for the will contest. Thus, contestants lose out only if it is determined that they challenged the will without good cause; if the will genuinely seems improper, they have less to lose by bringing the contest.

Under New York's statute, an *in terrorem* clause is valid and enforceable even if there is probable cause for the challenge—unless the challenge is based on forgery, revocation by a later will (and if this allegation is based on probable cause), unless the contestant is an infant or incompetent, or unless the objection is to the probate court's jurisdiction. Under the California statute, even if the will contains an *in terrorem* clause, any interested person may contest any provision of the will benefiting a *witness* without forfeiting his or her own portion of the estate, but in general, *in terrorem* clauses are valid under California law: *Estate of Black*, 206 Cal. Rptr. 663 (1984).

In terrorem clauses are not triggered by objections to the appointment of a particular executor: *Wojtalewicz v. Waitel*, 93 Ill. App. 3d 1061, 418 NE2d 418 (1981).

At least one state has held that *in terrorem* clauses are favored by public policy, because they reduce the burden of specious cases on the courts: *Matter of Estate of Westfahl*, 675 P.2d 21 (Okla. 1983). However, even this case requires the *in terrorem* clause to be enforced as written, strictly construed to prevent forfeitures if possible, and interpreted reasonably in favor of the beneficiary.

Other states have described *in terrorem* clauses as disfavored, and require strict construction: see, *Linkous v. National Bank of Georgia*, 247 Georgia 274, 274 SE2d 469 (1981); *Ivancovich v. Meier*, 122 Az. 346, 596 P.2d 24 (1979); *Estate of Alexander*, 395 NYS2d 598, 90 Misc.2d 482 (Surr. 1977).

Texas and Wyoming have recent case law indicating that these states do not have a "good faith and probable cause" exception to the rule that *in terrorem* clauses are enforceable: *Dainton v. Watson*, 638 P.2d 79 (Wyoming 1983); *Gunter v. Pogue*, 672 SW2d 840 (Texas 1984). *Gunter* says that the contestants didn't prove that they were operating in good faith with probable cause, even if such an exception existed.

A recent Oklahoma case, *Matter of Estate of Zarrow,* 688 P.2d 47 (1984), holds that a no-contest clause will not be enforced against the principal beneficiary when the intent of the will, as determined by construing the entire will, is to protect the principal beneficiary against the greed of the other beneficiaries.

Kyker v. Kyker, 117 Ill. App. 3d 547, 72 Ill. Dec. 808, 453 NE2d 108 (1983), holds that voluntary acceptance of benefits under a will (such as taking a check for a bequest) operates as ratification of the will, and thus precludes most challenges—but not challenges alleging a violation of law or public policy. Also see *Sheffield v. Scott,* 620 SW2d 691 (Tex. 1981), barring the testator's nephew and niece from contesting the testator's will; having accepted some of the property bequeathed to them, they were no longer "interested parties." Whether or not they knew all the facts when they accepted the property, they didn't try to give it back.

Two recent California cases deal with the applicability of the rule about no-contest clauses to actions other than conventional will contests. The earlier case is *Estate of Black,* 160 Cal. App. 3d 582, 206 Cal. Rptr. 663 (1984), holding that a no-contest clause will not penalize the testator's cohabitant for bringing a *"Marvin"*-type action asserting an implied partnership in the deceased testator's assets. The rationale was that, if the challenge was valid, the assets in question belonged to her anyway, and were not a proper subject for the testator's will.

The later case, *Estate of Larsen,* 207 Cal. Rptr. 526 (1984), interprets a suit on a creditor's claim for lifetime services to the testator as an indirect attack on the will, because a successful claim would frustrate the testator's intent. Thus, the beneficiary would suffer the effect of *in terrorem* clause, which was enforced by the court.

The New Mexico case of *Matter of Hilton,* 98 NM 420, 649 P2d 488 (1982), upholds an interesting technique that combines an *in terrorem* clause with a clause to eliminate pretermitted heir claims. The testator's will included a clause, "I declare that I have only three children: namely, Loretta Szaloy, Ara Cardin and Laura Griffin, my daughters, and that if any other person claims to be a child or heir of mine and establishes such claim in a Court of competent jurisdiction, I give to such person the sum of One Dollar." The nominal bequest would prevent them from being pretermitted heirs; if they accepted the dollar, they would be precluded from contesting the will. The court's rationale was that the testator expressly manifested his intent to disinherit everyone (including the children of one of his daughters, who predeceased him) who was not specifically mentioned in the will.

EXAMPLE: Paul Delahaye, a wealthy man, has never been married, but he has cohabited for many years with Tanya Loomis. Tanya's husband deserted her shortly after their marriage, and she has never bothered to get a divorce. Delahaye and Loomis have a cohabitation agreement, though they are not sure what force it would have in court.

Delahaye's relatives have always expressed the strongest possible disapproval both of Loomis and of the relationship. This has, understandably, caused friction within the family, but Delahaye does not want to exclude his closest relatives from his will entirely. However, he wants to make sure that the bulk of his estate will go to Loomis. Therefore, his will includes moderately generous provisions for his siblings (or their children, if his siblings predecease him)—but an *in terrorem* clause, with a gift over to Dartmouth College (Delahaye's alma mater), has been inserted to prevent his family from challenging the much larger bequests and devises to Loomis.

SUMMARY

Testators who wish to omit or limit provision for their spouses may do so by making adequate provision for the spouse outside the will; by executing a valid antenuptial agreement, based on full disclosure; or by getting a valid disclaimer of the right of election. In general, testators may exclude their children from inheritance by explicitly disinheriting certain children by name, or by specifying that no provision for children, whether living at that time or afterborn, is intended.

With the exceptions described above, testators may generally ensure that their wills cannot be challenged by including an *in terrorem* clause disinheriting those who institute or participate in will contests. ***PRACTICE TIP:*** *As a matter of good drafting, a will including an in terrorem clause must include a gift over in the event of a will contest.*

5

SPECIAL DRAFTING PROBLEMS

The will drafter faces many problems of language and expression. Superimposed on the heroic task of predicting the future—deciding what the testator will own at an indeterminate time, when he or she is either married or not, with surviving children or without them—are the problems of using terms that will be readily understood both by the testator and the probate court that will eventually hear the case, and constructing a testamentary scheme that conforms to the state of the law at the time of drafting.

THE "MAP"

There are many ways of organizing and drafting a will; in fact, there are many effective ways of handling this task. A very common "map" is to begin the will with an introduction, reciting the testator's name, marital status, citizenship, and domicile, and stating that this is his or her last will and that all earlier wills and codicils are revoked. Next, the conventional will proceeds with the appointment of fiduciary or fiduciaries; makes dispositive provisions (including any pourover to an existing *inter vivos* trust, or funding and management of a testamentary trust, if any); details the powers of the fiduciaries; disposes of the residue of the estate; and specifies "housekeeping" matters such as gifts over, simultaneous death provisions, and apportionment of any estate or inheritance tax due on the estate.

Another, less common but very useful method, is to begin with the usual recitals, then go on to a section of definitions. As we'll see below, the use of common English terms with accepted meanings can create enormous problems—what, for instance, is encompassed in a bequest of the "contents" of a desk, safe deposit box, or cardboard carton? Are sapphire-and-diamond cufflinks "clothing and personal effects?" ***PRACTICE TIP:*** *The drafter who anticipates such problems and includes a section of definitions can save the testator's family much anguish (and, very conceivably, can save him- or herself a malpractice suit).*

Strictly speaking, the balance between preresiduary and residuary dispositions is a matter of estate planning, not will drafting. But, of course, the will must include a residuary clause; if no such clause is included, part of the estate passes by will, part by intestacy: *In re Estate of Barker,* 448 So2d 28 (Fla. 1984). Furthermore, the residuary clause must be proportionate to the size of the residue that can reasonably be expected.

The case of *In re Cancik,* 106 Ill.2d 11, 87 Ill. Dec. 36, 476 NE2d 738 (1985), involved a very, very short will. The testator's personal effects were left to Cousin Charles; the residue was to fund a trust for care of the family mausoleum. The will said, "I have intentionally omitted the names of any of my relatives from this my last will and testament for reasons I deem good and sufficient, with the exception of my aforesaid cousin, Charles." But the estate was more than $200,000—quite a bit more than the mausoleum needed. The result was that Cousin Charles shared the amount not needed for upkeep with 12 Czech cousins who appeared out of the woodwork. ***PRACTICE TIP:*** *The lesson for the drafters is that it is not enough to exclude relatives from inheritance—there must be a provision that the estate go to someone.*

However, the drafter must be sensitive to the effect of changes in fortune on the testamentary scheme. The possibilities of abatement, ademption, and lapse (see Chapter 6 for a fuller discussion) are much greater if the bulk of the estate is disposed of before the residuary clause than if a few minor dispositions are made before the residuary clause, and the bulk of the estate is left to a specified group of people in specified percentages. (Of course, even under this scheme, there are problems of valuation and of allocating personal property.)

DEFINITIONS

Adoptees and Illegitimates

Two problems of definition are commonly settled by statute: the status of adopted children, and the status of illegitimate children, under gifts to "children," "grandchildren," "issue," and the like. In general, an adopted child *is* a "child" of his or her adoptive parents for purposes of both intestate inheritance and for taking under class gifts. The adoption ends the child's status as a *child* of his or her biological parents. See, *In re Best,* 54 LW 2265 (NY App. 1985) for example. (Of course, there is nothing to prevent the biological parents or their relatives from leaving money or property to children adopted into another family.) Alabama provides that, if a child is adopted by a natural parent's new spouse after a divorce and remarriage, the child will continue to be a "child" of the other biological parent.

Under California statute, children of the half blood, adopted children, foster children, and stepchildren born out of wedlock are included in class gifts unless the will is to the contrary. However, if the will in question is not that of the parent, a person is not considered the child of his or her natural parent unless he or she was brought up by the natural parent, the natural parent's sibling, or surviving spouse. This is also true of adopted persons where the testator is not the adoptive parent.

In general, an illegitimate child is considered the child of his or her mother, and is considered the child of his or her father if the father acknowledges the relationship, if the child is eventually legitimated by a marriage between the natural parents, or if there is a paternity order establishing the relationship.

PRACTICE TIP: As a rule, it is best for the drafter to specify whether adopted and illegitimate children are included or excluded in class gifts. The term "issue" is traditional, but problematic. The term "issue" is more or less equivalent to "heirs of the body," and can be construed to require direct biological descent. Because of the possibility of confusion, the drafter should choose other terms.

Consider the case of *Lehman v. Corpus Christi National Bank,* 668 SW2d 687 (Tex. 1984). The will included adoptees in the class of "descendants," so a person adopted as an adult was comprised in the class of descendants. The drafter of the will testified that the testator did not consider adult adoptees "descendants," but the court ruled that this testimony should not have been admitted: first because the will was not ambiguous, and second because of the difficulty of testifying to another person's state of mind.

Compare, for instance, the cases of *Evans v. McCoy,* 436 A2d 436 (Md. 1981) [absent evidence to the contrary, adoptees are "issue"]; *Estate of Riley,* 446 A2d 903 (Pa. 1982), [same]; *Skoog v. Fredell,* 332 NW2d 333 (Ia. 1983), [unless they show an intent to the contrary, it is presumed that strangers to an adoption will not distinguish between a person's natural children and his or her adopted children]; with *Estate of Tower,* 470 A2d 568 (Pa. 1983), [the testator did not intend to benefit adoptees, because the will evidenced a concern for the testator's own bloodline through repeated references to "children," "grandchildren," "issue," and "lineal descendants."], and *Vicars v. Mullins*, 318 SE2d 377 (Va. 1984) [a gift to children, sons, daughters, or issue benefits legitimate descendants only, and "issue" includes adoptees only if the intent to benefit them is express, reasonably implied from the language of the will, or reasonably inferred by the court based on admissible extrinsic evidence]. The term "issue" can also be interpreted to cover all subsequent generations; whether this will be done can depend on the intent of the testator, for example, *Chicago Title & Trust Co. v. Schwartz*, 120 Ill. App.3d 324, 458 NE2d 151 (1983): the will provided that the "issue" of a deceased legatee would take the parent's share. This was interpreted to mean the children of the deceased legatee only, not more remote descendants.

Many class gifts are gifts of a specific sum of money or item of fungible property (for example, $500 to each of my grandchildren who survives me). If the gift is in this form, the only potential problem is that the estate may be too small to satisfy all gifts (in which case, see the discussion of abatement on pages 113–117). A class gift may also take the form of percentages of a fund, or of the residue of the estate, in which case, there is a real possibility that the percentages will exceed one hundred if the class is a large one! A will speaks as of the date of the testator's death, so, unless the will is to the contrary, the size of the class if determined at the testator's death: *In re Criss' Trust*, 329 NW2d 842, 213 Neb. 379 (1983).

As always, the drafter must be aware of possible misinterpretations, and must redraft to eliminate them. Compare *Matter of Ross*, 424 NYS2d 661 (1980), [the residuary clause benefited "the children of my two nephews," one of whom had two children, the other had three; each took one-fifth, because the controlling statute provides that, absent express testamentary language, a class gift to those with an equal relationship to the testator is a per capita gift] with *Matter of Waskawic*, NYLJ 1/17/80 p. 16 [residuary estate divided "in equal shares to my children and to my wife's children" passed half the residue to the testator's two children, half to the four children of the testator's wife; for each to take 1/6, the clause would have to have read, "To my children and my wife's children, in equal shares.] Drafters, as well as diplomats, have to worry about orders of precedence.

Gift to a Person and Spouse

Sometimes a testator will want to leave something to a person and his or her spouse, or to make separate gifts to a person and his or her spouse. Given current high divorce rates, such a gift can create problems: it is not unlikely that the then-spouse will no longer be the spouse at the time of the testator's death. Even more confusing, someone who was married to Anne when the will was drafted can be married to Lucille when the will becomes effective. ***PRACTICE TIP:*** *The general rule is that a bequest to a person's spouse is the person he or she was married to at the execution of the will ("To my nephew Edward and his wife, I leave the sum of $1,000 each"); the bequest to a person or his or her surviving spouse, or to the "widow" or "widower" of a named person is the person married to the named person when he or she dies; and a bequest to* *a named person goes to him or her regardless of marital status ("I leave my son Richard and his wife Edna 500 shares of AT&T stock each"). But see Florida's In re Estate of McGlone, 436 So2d 441 (1983), which holds that, absent proof of contrary intent, a bequest to somebody and spouse or the survivor of them is not abated by the couple's divorce.*

*   **PRACTICE TIP:** Don't forget that a reference in a will to the "marital deduction" is interpreted to mean the law in effect at the testator's death, not that in force at the time the will was executed—another good reason for regular review and updating of wills! (Estate of Weeks, 462 A2d 44 (Me. 1983).*

Personal Property

Some of the most difficult problems in will drafting involve dispositions of the testator's miscellaneous personal property. (The problem is rather akin to the "floating lien" in secured transactions.) Few testators can give an accurate account of their ownership of assorted items, with small or moderate individual value but, frequently, significant collective value. Naturally, a person's wardrobe, household furnishings, or collections will change over time; so even if the testator is minutely accurate about everything that he or she owns when the will is written, the property collection will be different at the time of death.

One way to handle the problem is to have the testator make provision for particularly valuable items (automobile, antique furniture, precious jewelry), with due attention to the problems of lapse and ademption, then leave all his or her miscellaneous personal property to his or her spouse. This avoids the necessity of characterizing various small items as having belonged to the testator or the surviving spouse; and the surviving spouse will probably make a disposition of certain of the items with sentimental value more or less as the testator would have done.

Another approach is to use what might be called the "personal property letter," a device authorized by the statutes of Alaska, Arizona, Arkansas, Colorado, Delaware, Florida, Hawaii, Idaho, Iowa, Kansas, Maine, Michigan, Minnesota, Missouri, Montana, Nebraska, Nevada, New Jersey, New Mexico, North Dakota, Utah, and Washington. These states follow the doctrine of incorporation by reference, and permit a document disposing of personal property to be incorporated by reference into the will, even if the letter is not executed with testamentary formalities. Although the definition of the kinds of property that can be controlled by the letter differ from state to state (cites are given in the Table of Statutes), in general the restriction is to tangible, nonbusiness personal property, and securities and evidences of indebtedness are excluded.

The personal property letter can be changed as often as the testator wishes, without the need for scheduling another visit to the drafter's office. (The testator must be fully educated about the potential scope of the letter, and must alert the executor as to where the letter can be found.) The letter can be redrafted to add another piece of property newly acquired; to remove property that has been destroyed or sold; or to change dispositions if the original recipient has offended the testator or if the testator wishes to be more generous to the recipient.

Naturally, if the will refers to a personal property letter, the testator must be careful to leave such a letter! Consider the case of *Matter and Schmidt's Estate*, 638 P.2d 809 (Colo. 1981). The will provided that "tangible personal property" was to be disposed of according to the "memorandum which I intend to leave at my death," or, if there was no such memorandum, the legatee was to receive "whatever items of my personal property she chooses." The testator died without leaving such a memo; the court held that the devise was limited to items of personal property that could have passed under a "personal property letter"; the Colorado statute excluded money, evidences of indebtedness, documents of title, securities, and trade and business property from coverage, so the legatee was not entitled to receive bank accounts, credit union accounts, or insurance proceeds.

PRACTICE TIP: Here is yet another solution. The drafter can set up a scheme for disposition of miscellaneous personal property. All the miscellaneous property not otherwise disposed of can be placed in a group or lot, and divided into shares, with one share each going to a group of named persons. Or, various named persons can be given the option of selecting a certain number of items from the group (in the interest of harmony, it helps to specify the order in which the people can make their selections). In the interest of fairness, the executor can be given some "referee" power to make sure the choices are of roughly equal value. In the alternative, the executor can be given the power to select the items of property to be apportioned to the named recipients; or the executor can be given the task of dividing the items into a certain number of shares of approximately equal value. Under this approach, either the executor assigns the shares to the recipients (who can, of course, exchange items among themselves if they're unhappy with the executor's selection) or the recipients are allowed to choose the shares they prefer.

Drafters who also serve as executors must be warned that the process of disposing of property of quite limited financial or aesthetic value can give rise to endless hostility and controversy. Even if the drafter will not be serving as executor, it is wise to provide in the will that the discretion of the executor is final.

If a will is so poorly drafted that it must be construed by a court, the general principle of *ejusdem generis* is applied: that is, where words of a general nature follow, or are used in connection with the enumeration of objects or classes, the meaning of the general words will be limited to the particular words." When this principle is applied, "rings, brooches, and jewelry" will be construed to limit jewelry to rings and brooches. To avoid the application of *ejusdem generis*, use language such as "all my personal effects, including but not limited to clothing, furs, jewelry, etc."

In states that do not permit incorporation by reference of a personal property letter, or in estate plans for which this device is not suitable, the drafter must be especially careful about definitions; many will contests have turned on small points of language.

It has been held that a bequest of "$800,000 cash or stock" to a named legatee is a bequest of $800,000, which the legatee can take in either form (*Succession of Kearl*, 440 So.2d 179 (Louisiana 1983). "All the stock standing in my name at the time of my decease" does not include the shares of stock evidencing ownership of a co-op apartment; the apartment passed as part of the residue: *Estate of Strauss,* NYLJ 8/27/82 p.7. And a bequest of "1,000 shares computed on the basis of present value" means that the beneficiary doesn't get stock splits or dividends: *Re Estate of Hannon,* 447 So2d 1027 (Fla. App. 1984).

The devise of a house "including the contents thereof" includes the furniture and furnishings but not savings accounts, checking accounts, bonds, or uncashed checks found in the house (*Lamb Estate,* 445 Pa. 323, 285 A.2d 163 (1971). The devise of a house and garage and "furnishings within said house" does not include stock certificates, the title to the automobile, a mortgage payable to the testator, all found in the testator's safe inside the house, or the automobile itself that was parked in the garage. After all, the testator had not left the "contents" of the garage, and none of the instruments in the safe fit into any commonly accepted definition of "furnishings." (*In re Estate of Baker,* 495 Pa. 522, 434 A.2d 1213 (1981).

Yet another Pennsylvania case, *Matter of Estate of Rudy,* 329 Pa. Sup. 477, 478 A.2d 879 (1984), holds that cash, stocks, bonds, rare coins, watches, and jewelry are not "contents" of the house; instead, they fall under the definition of "personal effects" (left to someone other than the legatee of the "contents.")

In re Macfarlane's Estate, 459 A.2d 1289 (Pennsylvania 1983) is similar: the bequest of "tangible personal property" to the testator's wife included gold and silver coins, so she, rather than the charitable trust that was the residuary legatee, was entitled to the coins. A recent Alaska case, *Wlk v. Wlk,* 681 P.2d 336 (Alaska 1984), holds that a bequest of "all personal property" to the testator's son included a commercial fishing permit (even though the permit was acquired after the will was drafted) and thus would defeat a state statute passing the permit to the permit-holder's surviving spouse in the absent of contrary intent. Therefore it is good drafting procedure to make specific provision for such valuable licenses and permits.

A bequest of "personal effects, jewelry and furniture" has been held to pass the testator's silverware, on the theory that the testator's intention was to divide the estate between tangibles and intangibles: *Landstrom v. Krettler,* 435 NE2d 149 (Ill. App. 1982). Under *Matter of Geis' Estate,* 132 Ariz. 350, 645 P.2d 1264 (1982), jewelry that was often worn by the testator though it was kept in a safe deposit box passed under a bequest of "personal effects and other similar tangible personal property"; there was no dispute that jewelry kept in the testator's home would be considered personal effects.

A bequest of "all my personal property and household goods" was construed by *Sandy v. Mohout,* 1 Oh.St.3d 143, 438 NE2d 117 (1982), to pass $97,000 in intangible personal property. This did not leave much of a residue, but the court found that the testator's residuary clause served other purposes (for instance, dealing with the possibility that the niece would predecease the testator). Extrinsic evidence was also admitted, to show that the niece lived with the testator, and the residuary legatees were geographically as well as personally distant.

A money market savings certificate and a certificate of deposit not otherwise mentioned in the will passed under a bequest of "personal checking and savings accounts," because these instruments had the characteristics of savings accounts, and the court felt it was improper to penalize the testator for attempting to maximize the rate of return (*Gadoury v. Caldwell*, 425 So.2d 220 (Florida 1983)). Similarly, "cash in banks or otherwise" has been construed to include savings certificates (*Odom v. Odom*, 235 SE2d 29 (Ga. 1977)).

A recent New York case takes the position that the phrase "cash on hand" means demand funds, and includes the checking account: *Estate of Farone*, NYLJ 5/10/85 p.1 (Court of Appeals). "Any and all cash and jewelry" has been held to include bank accounts: *Estate of Cunningham*, NYLJ 5/12/75 p. 16; and "cash and bank accounts owned by me" to include a credit union account, but not the testator's balance in the state retirement fund: *In re Estate of Graham*, 419 P2d 97 (Ariz. 1966).

Silverthorn v. Jennings, 620 SW2d 894 (Tex. 1981), involved a will bequeathing the contents of a cardboard box in the testator's safe deposit box to one of her daughters, and the "remaining items" in the box to her other daughter. A certificate of deposit found in the safe deposit box, but not in the cardboard box, was held to belong to the second daughter; a CD is certainly an "item." There was no need to apply rules of construction, because the will was clear.

In cases of ambiguity in the terms of the will, extrinsic evidence may be admitted to clarify the testator's intent, for example, *Griffin v. Gould*, 60 Ill. Dec. 132, 432 NE2d 1031, 104 Ill. App. 3d 397 (1982). In this case, the testator bequeathed "jewelry, wearing apparel, silver, silverware, china, pictures, paintings, books and articles of household or personal use"; the case was remanded for evidence on the proper disposition of six statues, one kept in the testator's club, five kept in his home. But in *Martin v. First National Bank of Mobile*, 412 So.2d 250 (Alabama 1982), the admission of extrinsic evidence was held improper because there was no latent ambiguity in a bequest of "cars, trucks, and items of household property, personal property, and other items of personal property used in my every day life." The executrix had full power and authority to decide what property belonged within those classifications, so testimony was not necessary.

MALPRACTICE TRAPS

At first, lawyers could smile smugly, knowing that malpractice actions were unlikely to arise out of will drafting, even egregiously botched will drafting. The actual client, after all, would be dead, and the beneficiaries and intended beneficiaries would not have privity of contract with the attorney. However, in many states, it is now reasonably clear that negligent mistakes in will drafting can give rise to a malpractice action by the testator's intended beneficiaries; as *Lucas v. Hamm*, 56 Cal.2d 583, 587, 15 Cal. Rptr. 821, 825, 364 P.2d 685, 689 (1961), *cert. den.* 368 US 987 says:

The main purpose of the testator in making his agreement with the attorney is to benefit the persons named in his will and this intent can be effectuated, in the event of a breach by the attorney, only by giving the beneficiaries a right of action.

However, the lawyer won the case; the court held that a mistake in failing to avoid the rule against perpetuities was not malpractice, because lawyers often make such mistakes. Compare this case with *Millwright v. Romer,* 322 NW2d 30 (Iowa 1982), which held that a negligence action for preparing a will violating the rule against perpetuities accrues at the death of the testator (while the testator is alive, he or she has the option of having a better-drafted will prepared). To the *Millwright* court, everyone is presumed to know the law, and ignorance is no defense—least of all for an attorney. (Remember Jeremy Bentham's observation that lawyers are the only persons in whom ignorance of the law is not punished—and remember the film *Body Heat,* which shows the severe consequences of violating the Rule Against Perpetuities.)

There is substantial authority that those whom the testator intended to be beneficiaries, but who are omitted through the drafter's error, have an action against the drafter as third-party beneficiaries of the attorney-client contract. See, for example, the *Lucas* case cited above; *Woodfork v. Sanders,* 248 So2d 419 (Louisiana App. 1981); and *Guy v. Liederbach,* 279 Pa. Super. 543, 421 A.2d 333 (1981). A tort action may also lie: *Lucas, Licata v. Spector,* 26 Conn. Sup. 378, 255 A.2d 28 (1966).

Both tort and contract claims on the part of third-party nonclients were recognized in *Ogle v. Fuiten,* 112 Ill. App. 3d 1068, 68 Ill. Dec. 491, 445 NE2d 1344 (1983). The drafter negligently failed to deal with a contingency that did, in fact, occur, resulting in intestacy.

With regard to the presumption that a testator executes his will with knowledge of its contents, we do not believe that this is the same as concluding a testator knows whether this will will operate to effectuate his intentions. [...] A proper allegation of duty necessary to sustain a nonclient's action against an attorney for malpractice requires an allegation that the intent of the client to benefit the nonclient third party was the primary or direct purpose of the transaction or relationship. [445 NE2d at 1347-8]

The case of *Bucquet v. Livingston,* 57 Cal. App. 3d 914, 129 Cal. Rptr. 514, 518 (1976), deserves close attention. *Inter vivos* trust beneficiaries were found to have a malpractice cause of action on the grounds that the lawyer-drafter had negligently failed to advise the trust settlor about the tax consequences. According to the court, the case might not have been actionable if very complex issues had been involved (because the mistake would have been less likely to have been negligent), but a cut-and-dried marital deduction trust did not create such doubt.

An attorney may be liable to testamentary beneficiaries only if the stated test is fully met, that is, if due to the attorney's professional negligence the testamentary intent in a legal instrument is frustrated and the beneficiaries clearly designated by the testator lose their legacy as a direct result of such negligence.

In contrast, *Favata v. Rosenberg* 436 NE2d 49 (Ill. App. 1982), does not permit a third-party action by the intended beneficiaries of a badly drafted land trust; in this situation (perhaps because the client him- or herself is in a position to complain), the attorney's duty is owed only to the client, not to other people. Also see *Maneri v. Amodeo*, 38 Misc.2d 190, 238 NYS2d 302 (1963) [an attorney will be liable to a nonclient third-party only if guilty of fraud, collusion, or malicious acts; negligence—poor will drafting—will not give rise to a third-party action]; *Estate of Douglas*, NYLJ 4/9/80 p. 10 [the balance of equities does not favor discarding the traditional requirement of privity for attorney liability; case involved alleged negligence in the attorney's handling of a contested probate case.]

All these cases deal with mistakes of law made by drafters; *In re Estate of Pedrick*, 482 A2d 215 (Pennsylvania 1984), takes up the question of possible unethical action by the drafter. The attorney in question prepared a will with himself as one of the beneficiaries, in violation of the Code of Professional Conduct. The will was not invalidated, because the Code is not substantive law; however, the court declined to enforce the provisions in favor of the lawyer, because he came to court with unclean hands. Compare *Pedrick* with *In re Conduct of Tonkon*, 642 P2d 660 (Ore. Sup. 1982) [disciplinary charge dismissed against drafter-beneficiary of $75,000 of a $6,000,000 estate of a testator of somewhat impaired mental capacity] and with *In re Disciplinary Action Against Prueter*, 359 NW2d 613 (Minn. Sup. 1984) [attorney reprimanded for drafting a will naming himself as a major beneficiary].

PRACTICE TIP: Drafters should be aware that drafting a will benefiting themselves may lead to a presumption of undue influence if the will is challenged. The simple solution, if the bequest is larger than the fee, is to refer the grateful client to another attorney for preparation of the will.

No presumption of undue influence arises from an attorney-draftsman's service as executor of a will. However, if the attorney and his wife are co-executors and co-trustees, getting double commissions, this can be construed as tantamount to making the drafter a beneficiary—particularly as, in this case, there was a further suggestion of overreaching because the fiduciaries had the power to remove the corporate co-fiduciary and appoint a successor. Thus, the attorney was required to rebut the inference of undue influence and overreaching: *Estate of Becker* NYLJ 7/6/79 p. 15.

It is acceptable for the drafter to serve as a witness to a will, even if he is the executor of the will and a trustee of charities benefited by the will. A witness is not considered "interested" unless he or she has a pecuniary interest in the estate, and an executor merely has the right to receive reasonable compensation for services rendered: *Matter of Estate of Giacomini*, 4 Kan. App. 2d 126, 603 P2d 218 (1979).

In short, drafters have an obligation to study the substantive law of their state (and of any other state in which the testator owns property). They must either understand the income, gift, and estate tax consequences of the estate plan, or must retain co-counsel with this expertise. Nor may a drafter rest once an apparently valid will has been executed. Because the law changes dramatically over time, there is a continuing duty to correct the estate plan so that it continues to effectuate the testator's intention within the framework of current law.

In fact, the case of *Heyer v. Flaig,* 70 Cal. 2d 223, 74 Cal. Rptr. 225, 449 P.2d 161 (1969), finds a continuing tort in the failure to correct and update the estate plan. The effect of continuing tort is to prevent the statute of limitations from running against would-be plaintiffs.

Under *Heyer,* the statute of limitations against the beneficiaries who lose out because of the drafter's mistake does not start to run until the testator's death. The fact pattern is that the drafter knew that the testator was about to marry; her future husband was mentioned in the will, but only as an executor. He elected against the will, and the testator's children, who were supposed to receive her entire estate, sued the lawyer. The husband-executor also sued, but his claim was dismissed, because the estate was not really injured.

> A reasonably prudent attorney should appreciate the consequences of a post-testamentary marriage, advise the testator of such consequences, and use good judgment to avoid them if the testator so desires [...] Defendant owed a duty of care to the plaintiffs to effectuate in a non-negligent manner the testamentary scheme of the testatrix. Such a duty may extend beyond the date of the original drafting of the will when the attorney's negligent actions created a defective estate plan upon which the client might rely until her death. [449 P2d at pp. 165, 166]

The effect of this philosophy is to make it more imperative than ever for the attorney to keep in contact with estate planning clients until they definitely terminate the attorney's employment. ***PRACTICE TIP:*** *It always made good business sense to contact clients regularly, to educate them about changes in the law, and to inform them when changes in their estate plan were necessary. It may be necessary to do this to prevent charges of malpractice, or to prevail when such charges are made.*

COPING WITH CONTINGENCIES

At one extreme is the two-paragraph will that simply identifies the testator, appoints an executor, and leaves all of the testator's property to one named person, or a few named persons, with a gift over if they predecease. At the other extreme is the twenty-five-page will, with elaborate provisions for deaths by comet debris and destruction of property by sea monster.

The simple wills discussed in this book do not call for the latter approach, but the former is rather too casual. The drafter should be aware of, and should make provision for, the following:

- the marriage of an unmarried testator
- the divorce and possible remarriage of a married testator
- divorce and possible remarriage of a beneficiary

- the birth of (more) children to the testator
- if there are class gifts, the birth of more class members
- changes in the property owned by the testator
- changes in the value of property that continues owned by the testator until his/her death
- changes in tax rates
- changes in deductibility of items
- changes in the treatment of capital gains
- altering the characterization of an item from taxable to nontaxable, or vice versa
- changes in the testator's feelings toward a beneficiary or potential beneficiary who is not mentioned in the will
- simultaneous death of the testator and one or more beneficiaries
- one or more beneficiaries or fiduciaries predeceasing the testator
- one or more fiduciaries refusing to serve; dying while serving; or wishing to serve but being unable to qualify
- the possibility that the testator's spouse will die first
- the possibility that the testator's spouse may survive, but may die without appointing a guardian while there are still minor children.

The provisions need not be elaborate, simply an acknowledgment that the contingencies may happen, and a simple gift over or ademption provision; a designation of successor fiduciaries; and the like. See, for example, *Estate of Scheer,* NYLJ 10/16/80 p. 12. The testator's will provided that the residue was to go to the testator's grandchildren if the testator and his wife died simultaneously or as a result of common disaster. Instead, the testator's wife predeceased him, so the testator died intestate, because the contingency that really did occur was not provided for.

Just think how different literature (and jurisprudence) would have been if, in *The Merchant of Venice,* Shylock's lawyer had demanded security of a pound of flesh, and "appurtenant blood, bone, tissue, fluids, and other associated bio-materials." The moral? **PRACTICE TIP:** *Examine the will carefully to see what could go wrong between the time of drafting and the testator's death; and examine the will to see if there is anything that could be unclear to, or misconstrued by, parties who do not necessarily wish your client well.*

STYLE AND TONE

It is essential that clients (at least after proper education) be able to understand their wills, and to be sure that the will as drafted does reflect their desired disposition of property.

A concomitant of the axiom that a legal document should contain all that is essential to the intent of the parties is that it should likewise avoid meaningless recitations of language which by its lack of necessity can serve no purpose except to generate questions as to whether there exist some hidden reason for belaboring the instrument with the superfluous. Where legalisms are necessary and are intended to have impact on the provisions of the instrument, a challenge which the draftsman must meet is to reduce the requisite provisions to language that is commensurate with his client's level of education and comprehension. A failure to exhibit appropriate sensitivity to this necessity is to invite an issue as to the extent that the instrument is that of the testator or of only the draftsman. (*Matter of Estate of Hall*, 188 Misc.2d 1052, 462 NYS2d 154 (Surrogates' Court 1983).

On the understanding that "plain English" means suiting the level of writing to the client's needs, without sacrificing technical accuracy, all wills (and all other documents) should be in plain English. One way to resolve the conflict between simplicity and technical polish is to define all technical terms within the document, either in context as they occur or in a separate glossary at the beginning or end of the document.

Here are some other methods of turning traditional boilerplate into plain English.

- Go through the document and, if necessary, reorganize it, either structuring the document in chronological order (provisions dealing with the first step of the process are first, etc.); in order of importance (significant provisions first, collateral provisions later), or in another functional order.
- Replace archaic words with words in modern use, unless the archaic term is a legitimate term of art that permits a complex concept to be summed up quickly and accurately.
- Use frequent cross-references.
- Use examples wherever possible
- Give each section and subsection a heading, for quick reference. If this is done, it will no longer be necessary to search through an entire document to find a provision at issue.
- Try to replace long, complex sentences with a series of shorter sentences, or with a list in bulleted form, like this one.

The traditional distinction between "devises" of real property and "bequests" of anything else is eroding. However, in the sample clauses at the end of this book, I've preserved this usage. I've used terms like "legacy" (which can be either, or both) and verbs like "give" and "leave," which also can handle both situations. A common mistake in will drafting is to generalize from "I devise and bequeath my entire estate, both real and personal, to my spouse" (which is correct) and use the formula "devise and bequeath" for every separate disposition (which is wrong— you can't "devise and bequeath" a diamond necklace or an automobile).

Precatory Language

I suggest you avoid precatory language (that's a joke, folks). Precatory language (for example, "I suggest that she use this legacy to pay her medical school tuition") creates endless difficulties if the will must be construed. The line between a condition ("To my granddaughter Rachel, I leave the sum of $25,000 on condition that she is accepted to an accredited medical school on or before her 25th birthday, and that she enroll and complete at least one year of the course") and a precatory phrase can be difficult one to establish. If a condition *is* intended, this must be made very clear, and provision must be made for the failure of the condition.

Precatory language does have its place, for instance the so-called "secret trust": a person is left a legacy, and is to dispose of it according to the testator's intentions. Such a "secret trust" could be used to provide for a lover or an out-of-wedlock child; or, it could be a way of accomplishing the purposes served by the "personal property" letter previously discussed.

According to *Davis v. Davis*, 471 A2d 1008 (District of Columbia 1984), a "wish" directed to an executor is generally mandatory ("I suggest that my executor make all such payments and distributions within six months of my death"), a "wish" directed to anyone else is generally precatory. However, there is authority that designation of an attorney for the executor is precatory, not mandatory—the attorney-client relationship is too personal to be imposed on the executor by the testator's will: *Re Estate of Deardoff,* 10 Oh. St.3d 108, 461 NE2d 1292 (1984).

INCORPORATION BY REFERENCE

Most of the states (New York and Connecticut are conspicuous exceptions) follow the "English rule." That is, a document in existence at the time a will is executed can be incorporated into the will by reference—provided that the will refers specifically to the document and descibes it accurately enough to identify it. The will must *refer* to the document, physical attachment is not enough. See, for example, *Baxley v. Birmingham Trust Nat'l Bank,* 334 So2d 848 (Ala. 1976).

Two of the most important uses of this doctrine are the "personal property letter" and the "pourover." A pourover is a will provision directing that certain assets controlled by the will be added to the corpus of an *inter vivos* trust. Forty-two states (the cites can be found on page 102 of the 1985 pocket part of the *Uniform Laws Annotated*) have adopted the Uniform Testamentary Additions to Trusts Act. (The hold-outs are Alabama, Delaware, Louisiana, Missouri, Nebraska, Rhode Island, Virginia, and Wisconsin.) This Uniform Act permits a valid devise or bequest to the trustees of a trust created (or to be created) by the testator, even if the trust is unfunded, amendable, or revocable. If the trust *is* revoked or terminated during the testator's lifetime, the bequest or devise lapses.

SUMMARY

A good will drafter must be a good explainer. He or she must also be sensitive to language, and must provide clear definitions of potentially obscure or ambiguous terms such as "personal property." The drafter must decide which contingencies are reasonable and must be covered by the will, and which are too remote and would only burden the will with a weight of boilerplate. There must also be a continuing review of the estate plan to account for changes in material facts and substantive law (particularly tax law).

EXAMPLE: Beverly Dillon first became your client when she sued a former client of her commercial art studio over an unpaid bill. Since then, you took over the conduct of her divorce after she became embroiled in a dispute with the attorney originally handling the matter. In the course of that matter, you discovered that she did not have a will, nor did she have a partnership agreement with her partner in the studio. You drafted both these documents for her.

During the 1986 holiday season, you sent her a card giving both seasons' greetings and a few words about the revolutionary nature of the new law. In mid-1987, she made an appointment to review her will. During this review, you discovered that:

- the will disposes of her shares of stock appurtenant to a co-op apartment. However, she no longer owns the apartment; instead, she has purchased a nine-room house.

- She and her partner have dissolved the partnership, with only a moderate degree of acrimony, and the financial affairs of the partnership have been resolved—at the cost, however, of most of Beverley Dillon's cash, and some of the securities that she specifically bequeathed to her sister Eleanor.

- Now Dillon is the majority shareholder in Rapidograph Studios, Inc.

Her new will must cope with the fact that the co-op shares and securities are no longer in the estate, and must also dispose of the Rapidograph shares (unless the corporation, or the other shareholders, have a right of first refusal or positive obligation to purchase the shares). If the estate plan contained large cash bequests, the estate may be insufficient to pay them all unless Dillon replenishes her cash supply. Thus, the possibilities of both ademption and abatement must be addressed (see the next chapter).

6

SUBSTANTIVE ISSUES IN WILL DRAFTING

Apart from the substantive issues involved in choosing the appropriate estate plan for a client, the drafter will encounter a number of substantive issues in drafting itself. This chapter will give a brief summary of issues involved in assessing a client's testamentary capacity; handling dispositions to minor beneficiaries; handling charitable bequests; using the Uniform Simultaneous Death Act or reversing its presumption; and coping with the possibilities of abatement (estate insufficient to satisfy all legacies), ademption (estate no longer contains certain specifically disposed items), lapse (beneficiary predeceases testator), and apportionment of estate taxes.

Many of these issues are settled by state statutes; others depend on case law for their resolution.

TESTAMENTARY CAPACITY

A basic requisite of a valid will is that the testator must have testamentary capacity. In general, any adult who possesses property that may be disposed of by will is entitled to make a will. However, a person who suffers from severe mental or physical illness may not be able to comprehend the nature and extent of his or her property; may not recognize or be aware of the identity of relatives or friends; may suffer from delusions making it impossible for him or her to make a valid will.

Unless the testator possessed testamentary capacity at the time he or she made the will (or amended it by codicil), the will or codicil is invalid from the inception. Of course, a will can also be invalid if a person who possesses testamentary capacity is defrauded or subjected to duress or undue influence.

A few states have addressed the issue of testamentary capacity by statute. Reasonably enough, older people are more likely to make wills than younger people, and it is a well-known fact that some (although by no means all) people develop hardening of the arteries of the brain, Alzheimer's Disease, or other conditions affecting their mental capacity. Thus, the major issue of testamentary capacity involves the capacity of older persons, especially those who have been medically diagnosed or informally labeled as "senile."

Georgia has an especially elaborate statutory scheme (§§ 53-2-21—53-2-25). This state defines testamentary capacity as a decided and rational desire to make a disposition of property, and specifies that testamentary capacity can exist without contractual capacity. (That is, the requirements of testamentary capacity are narrower.) An insane person can make a valid will during a lucid interval; a "monomaniac" can make a valid will if the will is unconnected with the monomania (for example, a person who is sure that extraterrestrials are broadcasting through his or her bridgework can make a valid will devoid of references to the extragalactic menace). Section 53-2-25 is especially interesting for our purposes:

> (a) eccentricity of habit or thought does not deprive a person of the power of making a will.
>
> (b) old age and weakness of intellect resulting therefrom does not, of itself, constitute incapacity to make a will; however, if such weakness amounts to imbecility, the testamentary capacity is gone. In cases of doubt as to the extent of a testator's weakness of intellect, the reasonable or unreasonable disposition of his estate should have much weight in the decision of the question.

In North Dakota (§30.1-08.1) and Ohio (§2107.081), antemortem probate is permitted, that is, a living testator can get a declaratory judgment on the validity of a proposed will, including his or her own testamentary capacity.

In the other states, it is necessary to look at the case law. The general principle seems to be to find capacity except in the most extreme cases. Testamentary capacity has been defined as knowledge of one's estate; recognition of the natural objects of one's bounty; and having a dispositive scheme for one's property. The degree of capacity involved is less than that required to handle everyday business affairs. See, for example, *In re Hastings' Estate,* 479 Pa. 122, 387 A2d 865 (1978); *Matter of Congdon's Estate,* 309 NW2d 261 (Minnesota 1981, adding the refinement that the testator must be able to hold these things in mind long enough to form a rational judgment); and *Estate of Rosen,* 447 A.2d 1220 (Maine 1982).

Old age, physical weakness, even "senile dementia" are not necessarily inconsistent with testamentary capacity, as long as the testator was acting rationally when the codicil in question was prepared and executed, *Matter of Hedges,* 473 NYS2d 529 (1984). "Mild to moderate senile dementia" was held insufficient to overcome the strong presumption of sanity in *Succession of Catanzaro,* 417 So2d 863 (Louisiana 1982). Similarly, the Kansas case of *Matter of Brown's Estate,* 640 P2d 1250 (1982) holds that senile dementia (sequelae of cerebral arteriosclerosis) is not necessarily equivalent to a lack of testamentary capacity.

A diagnosis of "cerebral sclerotic confusion" and a doctor's "impression" of senile dementia did not invalidate the will at issue in *Wall v. Haller,* 486 A2d 764 (Maryland 1985), where there was no evidence of permanent insanity at the time of signing, and the will seemed to reflect the wishes of the testator, who in turn seemed to know what he was doing.

The term "senility" is not a scientific or medical term, and it can include the effects of a variety of mental illnesses and organic diseases of the brain. (The term can also reflect prejudice against old people; behavior that would be tolerated, or at worst described as "eccentric" in a younger person is often considered evidence of senility.) A diagnosis using the more scientific term "organic brain syndrome" does not automatically invalidate a will for lack of testamentary capacity, *Matter of Estate of Hastings,* 347 NW2d 347 (South Dakota 1984).

The 1977 case of *Evans v. Liston,* 116 Az. App. 218, 568 P2d 1116, provides an interesting extended discussion. Under this case, a senile person maintains testamentary capacity as long as he or she is not insane; to be invalid, the will must be the product of a delusion or hallucination.

> The fact that there exists a generally deteriorating mental condition or that old age is accompanied by mental slowness, poor memory, childishness, eccentricities and physical infirmities does not show lack of testamentary capacity. (Pages 1117-8).

As a final variation on the theme, consider *Matter of LaTray's Estate,* 183 Mont. 141, 598 P2d 619 (1979). The 79-year-old testator suffered from various physical health problems, and occasionally experienced confusion and disorientation. However, there was substantial evidence of competence at the time the will was made. Furthermore, it was similar to earlier wills, made at a time when the testator was unquestionably competent.

Timing Requirements

This brings us to the question of the time as of which testamentary capacity must be measured. It is well-settled law that testamentary capacity must exist at the time the will is made; it is not necessary that the testator have been competent throughout his or her lifetime. See, for example, *Speck v. Speck*, 588 SW2d 853 (Texas 1979), *York v. Smith*, 385 So2d 1110 (Florida 1980), and *Matter of Yett's Estate*, 44 Ore.App. 709, 606 P2d 1174 (1980).

Evidence of incapacity a reasonable time before or after execution of the will (or codicil) may be admissible, but it will not be determinative of the existence or absence of testamentary capacity. See *Matter of Gentry's Estate*, 32 Ore.App. 45, 573 P2d 322 (1978), *In re Blakey's Estate*, 363 So2d 630 (Florida 1978), *In re Kuzma's Estate*, 487 Pa. 91, 408 A2d 1369 (1979), *Rich v. Rich*, 615 SW2d 795 (Texas 1980), and *York v. Smith*, 385 So2d 1110 (Florida 1980) [testamentary capacity required when the will is signed, not necessarily on the date when the testator acknowledges his or her signature before witnesses].

Everyone is presumed to be sane, and thus to have testamentary capacity; therefore, in a will contest, the burden is on the contestant to prove that the testator lacked testamentary capacity. *Fletcher v. DeLoatch*, 360 So2d 316 (Alabama 1978).

Guardianship and Conservatorship

Sometimes a mentally ill person, or an older person suffering from organic brain disease or enfeebled by age, will become the subject of a guardianship or conservatorship proceeding. (These are the most common terms; individual state terms may differ.)

Broadly speaking, conservatorship, or the appointment of a guardian of the property, is appropriate when a person is not able to manage financial affairs but is not so impaired as to merit a judgment of incapacity and restriction of civil rights. Guardianship, or appointment of a guardian of the person and property, is appropriate where the ward needs broader protection, and is unable to handle self-care, much less business affairs.

A number of cases indicate that the fact that a person is a conservatee does not preclude him or her from having testamentary capacity; nor must the conservatee get the consent of the conservator, or of the supervising court, to make a will. See *Thomas v. Hamlin*, 56 Tenn. App. 13, 404 SW2d 569 (1964), *Tucker v. Bowen*, 345 Mass. 27, 235 NE2d 896 (1968), *Lee v. Lee*, 337 So2d 713 (Mississippi 1976), *Estate of Letsche*, 29 Ill.Dec. 915, 392 NE2d 612, 73 Ill.App.3d 643 (1979), *Matter of Congdon's Estate*, 309 NW2d 261 (Minnesota 1981). The conservator has no power to set aside a conservatee's will during the conservatee's lifetime. The conservator's job is to manage the conservatee's assets—a will is not an asset: *Rubin v. United Methodist City Soc. Inc.*, *NYLJ* 12/28/81 p. 13.

Even guardianship, which is more restrictive of the ward, does not necessarily preclude the ability to execute a valid will. Each individual case must be examined. See, for example, *Parham v. Walker*, 568 SW2d 622 (Tennessee 1978), *In re Hastings' Estate*, 479 Pa. 122, 387 A2d 865 (1978), *Matter of Will of Maynard*, 307 SE2d 416 (North Carolina 1983), and *Harper v. Watkins*, 670 SW2d 611 (Tennessee 1984).

A recent Louisiana case, *Succession of Price v. Price*, 448 So.2d 839 (1984), involves a testator who was discharged from the Army on the grounds of "mental defect, moron" and who was "interdicted" (the local term for guardianship) in 1925 with a diagnosis of "dementia praecox—simple type." The interdiction was still in effect when he died in 1981. Nevertheless, his will was upheld on testimony of his physician and several other people as to his mental health.

The testator in *In re Kleeb's Estate*, 211 Neb. 763, 320 NW2d 459 (1982), suffered from an advanced case of Parkinson's disease. She was hostile toward her daughters, which perhaps is not surprising because they had instituted conservatorship and guardianship proceedings against her. The testator's son (and the beneficiary of the disputed will) had her examined by two doctors, who agreed that she had testamentary capacity. The day after the examination, the son took her to a lawyer's office, and the will was drafted. The will was upheld, on the grounds that the testator understood the process of will making, and, while she may have been prejudiced against her daughters, she was not behaving in an irrational fashion.

PRACTICE TIPS: What should you do if you have a client who is at least arguably impaired, and who wishes to make a will? (1) First of all, you should satisfy yourself that the client does meet the rather low standard of testamentary capacity. As I had discussed above, you will need to find out the extent of the client's property to do a proper job of will drafting. The necessary inquiries can also be a way of assessing the client's knowledge of his or her property. If you've represented the client in other contexts, you may have some independent knowledge. Is the client confidently willing away assets that were spent or sold years ago? On the contrary, is a prosperous testator (the purchase of whose expensive house, and subsequent satisfaction of the mortgage, you've handled) disposing of only a very limited portion of his or her assets?

(2) You'll also have to find out who the client's natural heirs are, if only to determine whether the spouse (if any) would have a right of election, and to find out if any applicable pretermission statutes have been avoided. You'll have a chance to see if the client's attitude toward these persons appears to be irrational. A dislike of a sibling or a child, even if based on prejudice (for example, a desire to disinherit a child who has married outside the parents' faith) or mistake (belief that a spouse is unfaithful) is not necessarily irrational.

(3) The drafter faces a possible "self-fulfilling prophecy": if he or she includes, in the file, letters from the client's physicians, or a specially retained consultant experienced in mental and organic brain problems of the elderly, he or she may find that doubt is created as to the testator's capacity. This is also a "Catch-22" situation; failure to obtain such evidence when the testator was alive and could be examined may lead to invalidation of the will, because will contestants may introduce evidence of lack of capacity that cannot be rebutted.

PRACTICE TIP: Sometimes, it is conceded by everyone that the testator is in fact mentally ill or impaired by aging. However, there may be a reasonable argument to be made that the testator experiences lucid intervals. This contention should be backed up by affidavits from expert physicians or psychologists. It will also be necessary to work closely with the experts and the testator's family (and perhaps administrators, if the testator is a hospital or nursing-home patient) to choose appointments at times when the testator is at his or her best. It may also be necessary to adjust the dosage of pain relieving or psychoactive medication the testator receives to allow him or her to concentrate more fully on financial affairs and estate planning. (Drugs for high blood pressure and heart ailments may also affect alertness and memory.)

Sometimes the testator has had a conservator or guardian appointed, or such proceedings may be pending. The appointment probably does not preclude the possibility of making a valid will (although it does increase the likelihood of a challenge if there are any sufficiently disgruntled potential heirs). Thus, it is not necessary for the drafter to oppose the appointment merely to preserve estate planning options (although there may be other valid reasons to oppose the appointment).

PRACTICE TIP: *Drafters with a fondness for high-tech devices can videotape the execution of wills and trusts, so that the testator's demeanor can be observed in a will contest or challenge to the validity of the trust. It is much better (although more expensive) to do this routinely; if it's reserved for exceptional cases, the presumption is created that the drafter was dubious about the validity of the document.*

ABATEMENT

A will is made at a particular time, when the testator can have a fairly accurate idea of his or her financial status *at that time*. The will does not become effective until the testator's death, at which time the financial situation can be quite different. As long as the will has an adequate residuary clause, the situation of a greatly *increased* estate creates few problems.

In the opposite case, however—where the estate has *decreased*—it is quite possible that the specific dispositions of money and property will exceed the gross estate. One way to cope with this is to state all dispositions (except, perhaps, for minor bequests of personal property) in percentage terms— the estate will always add up to 100 percent, after all.

However, an estate plan that represents both a fair provision for the testator's family and generous disposition to friends and charities when the estate is large, may mean deprivation for the family when the estate is small. Many states have abatement statutes specifying the disposition of the estate if the estate is insufficient to meet all the claims on it (including any applicable estate or inheritance tax). The exceptional jurisdictions—the ones without abatement statutes—are the District of Columbia, Illinois, Louisiana, Mississippi, New Jersey, Rhode Island, South Carolina, Tennessee, Vermont, Virginia, Washington, and West Virginia.

There are some terms to keep in mind when reading state statutes. A *specific legacy* is a bequest of a particular thing or an identifiable part of the testator's estate, described so it can be distinguished from other property of the same type. The bequest is satisfied only by delivering *that* property, subject to encumbrances. A *general* legacy is payable out of the testator's personal estate, with no distinctions made. A bequest of money, with no fund for payment specified, is a general legacy.

Also, unless particular shares are specified, a legacy of stock in a named corporation is a general legacy. A *demonstrative* disposition is charged against a particular fund, but with no intention to relieve the estate as a whole of liability if that fund is unavailable. States usually try to protect specific legacies from abatement; then general and demonstrative legacies.

Many of the other states provide for what could be called "1-2-3-4" abatement. That is, all dispositions are divided into classes. Abatement takes place only within a class, unless the will provides to the contrary. The first class to abate is property not disposed of in the will. Next, the residue will be reduced, if elimination of nontestamentary property still leaves unmeetable claims against the estate. Third, general dispositions (those that do not specify an item of property or a fund from which they will be paid, such as "$1,000 in cash or stock") abate. The last to abate are specific dispositions ("The sum of $5,000, to be paid from my account at the Third National Bank").

This is not the only statutory scheme for abatement. (Citations for all the statutes mentioned here will be found in the statute table.) Kansas provides a different four-step abatement process. Personal property not disposed of by will abates first, then real property not disposed of by will, then personal property to the residuary legatee, then real property to the residuary legatee. So Kansas, unlike most other states, shows an intention to protect the residuary legatee. Maryland has a seven-step process: first property not in the will, then the residue, then the general legacies, then general legacies to dependents of the testator, then general legacies to the testator's *creditors*, then general legacies to the surviving spouse. The last to abate, under the Maryland scheme, are specific and demonstrative legacies.

In Michigan, the residue will be reduced first; if it is eliminated, and the legacies still exceed the estate, then general or demonstrative legacies will abate before specific dispositions. New Hampshire requires the probate judge to handle abatement, directing that it be done "equitably."

The New York statute gives a particularly elaborate scheme: distributive shares in property not disposed of by will abate first. Next are residuary dispositions, then general dispositions. Demonstrative dispositions are treated as general dispositions to the extent the property or fund identified for payment has adeemed (is no longer in the estate). The fourth class to be abated are specific dispositions, in accordance with the beneficiaries' respective interests in the dispositions. Unadeemed demonstrative dispositions are treated as specific for this purpose. Last, dispositions to the surviving spouse qualifying for the marital deduction will abate—but only after all other classes of disposition have been abated.

Oklahoma does not specify an order, but provides that abatement takes place only within a class unless the will is to the contrary.

Wyoming has a five-step system: first, property not disposed of in the will abates, then the residue (except to the extent the residuary legatee is a surviving spouse taking under the will), then general and demonstrative dispositions, then specific dispositions to anyone other than the surviving spouse taking under the will. Specific dispositions to the surviving spouse taking under the will abate last of all.

None of these abatement schemes is mandatory; all may be varied by will. So the drafter must choose an abatement provision that fits the testator's estate plan, makes realistic allowance for the fact that older people, or those in poor health, are likely to predecease younger or healthier people, and copes with the economic realities of what is likely to happen to the testator's estate. An estate including a high proportion of blue-chip stocks and real estate in high-value areas is likely to increase in value (especially if the testator has taken steps to shield the estate against the high cost of custodial health care). However, if the estate consists of small savings accounts and a few investments, and if the testator must live on a small fixed income after retirement, the estate is very likely to diminish, or even be depleted, before the testator's death.

California's *Estate of Jenanyan,* 183 Cal. Rptr. 525, 646 P2d 196 (1982), permits a court to order abatement of a specific devise to pay debts, administration expenses, or the family allowance, or to adjust the estate for the interest of a pretermitted heir. However, a specific devise cannot be abated to satisfy a general legacy, unless there is affirmative, unequivocal evidence that this was the intention of the testator.

ANTILAPSE PROVISIONS

Sometimes beneficiaries predecease testators, and a wise drafter will make provisions for this possibility by providing for gifts over. If there is no gift over, many states treat the lapsed disposition as part of the residuary estate; however, some states will treat a lapse in the residue as partial intestacy. ***PRACTICE TIP:** The drafter must also educate the testator about the need to review the estate plan, and perhaps amend the will or make a new will, if a major beneficiary predeceases.*

If the drafter omits this step, nearly all the states (the frequently anomalous Louisiana is the exception) have antilapse statutes to protect the testator's relatives. If one of the testator's children (or, in some states, the issue of the testator's parents such as his or her siblings) is a beneficiary who predeceases the testator, the issue of the deceased beneficiary will inherit his or her share.

Thus, the antilapse statutes do not protect the legacies to the testator's live-in lover or friends; and, if the state antilapse statute's provisions are not in accord with the testator's estate plan, the testator must be careful to advise the drafter of his or her wishes.

A recent Missouri case, *Taylor v. Coe,* 675 SW2d 148 (1984), clarifies that an antilapse statute will not prevent the lapse of a disposition to a relative who does not leave any lineal descendents. This case deals with a legatee who was robbed and murdered at the same time as the testator, and thus also reiterates the principle that the Uniform Simultaneous Death Act requires the party who claims based on survivorship to prove that the beneficiary did, in fact, survive the testator.

SIMULTANEOUS DEATH

Most of the states have adopted the Uniform Simultaneous Death Act, with very minor state-to-state variations. (Cites in the table of statutes.) The holdouts are Alaska, Louisiana, Montana, and Ohio.

Under the Uniform Act,

> Where the title to property or the devolution thereof depends upon priority of death and there is no sufficient evidence that the persons have died other than simultaneously, the property of each person shall be disposed of as if he had survived, except as provided otherwise in this act. [Section 1]

Under the Uniform Act, if a beneficiary's right to inherit is contingent on his or her survival, he or she is deemed *not* to have survived, and the legacy contingent on survival will fail. If there are several beneficiaries and their order of death cannot be determined, the property left to all of them is to be divided into one equal share per beneficiary, and disposed of to those who would have taken if each beneficiary had in fact been the survivor.

Joint tenancy property, or property held by the entirety, passes half as if each owner had survived. (If there are several joint tenants whose survivorship cannot be determined, the property is divided into equal shares for each tenant; each tenant's share passes as if he or she had survived.) Similarly, if married owners of community property die and survivorship cannot be established, half passes as if each spouse had survived.

The Uniform Act also provides that if an insured and the beneficiary of the policy die more or less simultaneously, the proceeds of the policy are distributed as if the *insured* had survived. So it's particularly important for the policy to designate a contingent beneficiary.

All these provisions apply only if the will is silent. If one spouse is significantly more affluent than the other, it may serve important estate planning objectives to do as much as possible to equalize the estates. This can be achieved by reversing the presumption in the will of the richer spouse; that is, the estate of the richer spouse will pass as if the poorer spouse had survived. If the presumption is not reversed in the poorer spouse's will, his or her own property will also pass as if he or she had survived.

PRACTICE TIP: 1) Be careful to avoid creating a "loop" by setting up a scheme for a married couple in which each leaves all his or her property to the spouse, with no provision for alternate beneficiaries if the spouse predeceases or dies at approximately the same time. In this situation, each spouse is presumed to survive for the purposes of his or her own will, which passes the property to the spouse, who is presumed to predecease.

2) Drafters must also remember that the Uniform Simultaneous Death Act does not apply when there is in fact sufficient evidence to determine the order of two or more deaths (for example, when rescuers arrive on the scene and find one spouse dead and the other dying; when autopsy evidence establishes that one spouse drowned, but that the other spouse was dead when the vehicle entered the water).

3) A final point to remember: a simultaneous death provision is not identical to a "common disaster" clause; a "common disaster" clause may divest a legacy to someone who dies in a "common disaster" with the testator. However, common disaster clauses operate even if the beneficiary dies after the common disaster, as a result of it (for example, testator and beneficiary are passengers in a plane that crashes; the testator dies during the crash, and the beneficiary dies three days later, of crash-related injuries. In this situation, a common disaster clause would apply, but a simultaneous death provision would not, because it is clear that the testator died first.)

Here is another reminder of the difficulties one little word can create. The will in *Estate of Scott*, 604 P2d 864 (Okla. 1979), was drafted so that the testator's sister was to inherit his entire estate, "provided she survives me and we do not both die as the result of a common disaster or within (60) days from the date thereof..."; the gift over was to the testator's stepdaughter. The testator's sister did die within 60 days of his death, but not as a result of a common disaster. The court interpreted "thereof" to mean from the date of the (nonexistent) common disaster, and vacated the lower court decision and remanded for further proceedings.

EXONERATION

It's not uncommon for real property passing by will to be subject to a mortgage, nor for personal property to be encumbered by some type of security interest. So the drafter must ask the client for information about encumbrances on his or her property, and must be aware of the fact that the general rule is that the inheritor of encumbered property takes it "as is," subject to the encumbrances. This is true even if the will directs the executor to pay the testator's "just debts"; such a direction will not obligate the executor to satisfy mortgages or security interests.

Application of this rule can be altered by will, and the testator may want to provide a source of funds and direct the executor to pay off the encumbrances so the legatee can take the property free and clear.

Kansas has an unusual statute (§59-1304) permitting an executor or administrator to satisfy encumbrances, even if the will does not so specify, if this is in the best interests of the estate, by obtaining a court order. However, unless the will so provides, such a payment may not be used to increase any legatee's share of the estate. North Dakota §30.1-19-14 is similar.

Under Maryland statute (Estates & Trusts §4-406), legatees are entitled to exoneration of security interests that attached after execution of the will; as for security interests in effect when the will was executed, the property will pass encumbered unless the will specifies that it passes free and clear. The North Carolina law (§28A-15-3) specifies that property passes subject to liens and security interests—but not judgment liens—unless the will is to the contrary.

One possible approach is for the testator to provide that his or her immediate family are to take encumbered property free and clear, but all other legatees must take the property subject to the encumbrances.

Also see *In re Estate of Britt*, 112 Ill. App. 3d 186, 76 Ill. Dec. 952, 445 NE2d 367 (1983). The testator's wife was given "one third of my estate," with the residue in trust to the appellees. The court held that, under the "burden on the residue" rule with which attorneys are presumed to be familiar, if the will is silent, taxes, debts, and fees are expenses of administration, paid from the residue; therefore, the widow's one-third interest was free and clear.

APPORTIONMENT OF ESTATE TAXES

As you can see from the table of statutes, twenty-two states (Alaska, California, Colorado, Florida, Georgia, Idaho, Kansas, Louisiana, Maine, Maryland, Massachusetts, Michigan, Minnesota, Montana, Nevada, New York, North Dakota, Pennsylvania, South Dakota, Tennessee, Utah, and Virginia) have statutes dealing with the way estate tax will be apportioned if the will is silent.

In general, these statutes provide that estate tax is apportioned either "equitably" among all takers under the will, or proportionately to their interest in the estate; Pennsylvania charges inheritance tax to the residue as an expense of administration.

The drafter must make a tentative computation of whether federal estate tax and/or state inheritance and estate tax will be payable on the estate. If it seems likely that there will be such taxes, the drafter must make sure that the taxes will not lead to abatement of legacies; and must decide whether the statutory scheme fits in with the estate plan. If not, the drafter must decide who should bear the burden of the tax.

Frequently, the residue is burdened with the estate tax, unless, of course, the residue contains the bulk of the estate, and the testator's spouse and/or children are major residuary legatees. See, for example, *Wendland v. Washburn University*, 8 Kan. App. 2d 778, 667 P2d 915 (1983) [state inheritance tax, unlike federal estate tax, is a tax on the privilege of inheriting; to avoid statutory apportionment of tax among heirs, the testator—in this case a lawyer—must clearly indicate an alternative scheme]. Compare this with *Re Estate of Hawes*, 235 Kan. 697, 683 P2d 1252 (1984) [unless the will specifies, the burden of estate tax falls on the residue, not the surviving spouse's share qualifying for the marital deduction; if the residue is smaller than the tax, all beneficiaries must contribute, proportionately to their shares of the estate].

CHARITABLE BEQUESTS

The first task is to make sure that the testator has given you the correct name of the charity; frequently, there are several organizations with very similar names (and sometimes, with very different objectives and styles of administration).

Next, find out whether the organization is on the IRS's most recent list of qualified charitable organizations (and review the charitable bequests against the most current list whenever you perform a routine review of the will and estate plan, or whenever the will is amended in light of changed circumstances). Check with the client to find out what he or she prefers to do if, at any time, the charitable beneficiary no longer exists or is no longer a qualified charity for IRS purposes; does he or she want the bequest to go to the charitable organization's successor, or a completely different disposition to be made? See, for example, *Estate of Bernstrauch*, 210 Neb. 135, 313 NW2d 264 (1981). The bequest was to the (nonexistent) "Masonic Lodge for Crippled Children"; on *cy-pres* principles, the money was awarded to the "Shriners Hospital for Crippled Children" rather than the other claimant, the "Masonic Lodge." (*Cy-pres* is a medieval French legal expression meaning "as close as possible.")

EXAMPLE Theodore Goff, 74, has a chronic heart condition and has just been diagnosed as a victim of liver cancer. He knows this, and also knows that he must act quickly to implement any estate planning decisions. Goff is a widower, so the marital deduction will not be available to reduce the impact of estate tax on his estate (approximately $750,000). Goff also wants to benefit his two children, five grandchildren, and two great-grandchildren. The great-grandchildren, of course, are minors—and Goff probably does not have time to wait to see them grow up!

His immediate decision is to implement a giving program: $10,000 each to his children and their children and grandchildren, and to each of several charities. He estimates that this program, once the expenses of his last illness have been paid, will reduce the estate below the threshhold for federal estate tax. He has also had a new will drafted including testamentary trusts paying income for life to his grandchildren, with the principal then going to his great-grandchildren alive when the last of his grandchildren dies. He has left his collection of art to the nearest museum—and has arranged for it to be appraised during his lifetime. He has also checked with the museum; the gift is a welcome one. One of his great-grandchildren, eleven-year-old Willie Schulze, is the only one in the family to share his interest in coin collecting. Therefore, he wants Willie to get the (quite valuable) coin collection—this has been handled by bequeathing it to Willie's father, Eric Schulze, who understands that it is for Willie and will pass it along to him when, in Schulze's judgment, Willie is mature enough to take care of the valuable collection.

Charitable bequests should be reviewed for potential violation of law. Under certain circumstances, a very large charitable bequest may violate a "mortmain" statute forbidding "excessive" charitable bequests. Furthermore, bequests that are potentially violative of public policy should be reviewed, for example, a scholarship for "deserving young men of the Caucasian race"; establishment of a fund to provide for "needy members of the Presbyterian faith." However, New York has allowed a private trust to provide scholarships for "five young men" or "bright and deserving young men" over Equal Protection arguments (*Matter of Estate of Wilson,* 52 NY 461, 452 NE2d 1228, 465 NYS2d 900 (1983)).

Where a bequest violates public policy, it may be possible for the court hearing the challenge to re-form the bequest under the doctrine of *cy-pres*, perhaps by opening up the scholarship or the fund to the needy and deserving of any race or religion, female as well as male. The distinction may also turn on whether the bequest is to be administered by a private or a public body. In the latter case, the challenged provision is more likely to be invalidated.

Sticky issues can arise when the charitable bequest involves property rather than money—typically, the private papers of the testator, or some ancestor of whom he or she is particularly proud; a collection of family portraits; some furniture that is either priceless Federal antiques or Grand Rapids junk, depending on whether you accept the testator's opinion or the local museum curator's. In these situations, it makes a lot of sense to find out if the proposed recipient wants the stuff in the first place, and to find out if they intend to use the bequest or "deaccession" it (a diplomatic term for "sell this junk to raise some money to buy what we really want"). Once he or she finds out that the latter is the intention, the testator may prefer to give the material to another charitable beneficiary; to a noncharitable beneficiary (for example, keep the alleged heirlooms in the family); or direct that the material be sold during his or her own life or after death, and the proceeds of the sale distributed.

DISPOSITIONS TO MINORS

In addition to legal disabilities on their power to contract, there are very real practical difficulties; a minor (or even a young adult) is likely to lack the maturity to deal with large sums of money or valuable property.

As mentioned above, one of the most important functions of the will of a parent of young children is to designate a guardian for the children if both parents die simultaneously or within a short time, or if the surviving spouse dies while the children are minors, without designating a guardian.

If minors do inherit substantial assets, it will probably be necessary for a guardian to be appointed by the probate court (or other court with jurisdiction), a time-consuming proceeding. Furthermore, it may be necessary for the guardian to get court approval for major transactions involving the minors' property, not merely time-consuming but expensive and likely to consume much of the minors' property.

A traditional method of solving such problems is to make transfers to minors in trust, and permitting the trustees to make the required decisions and take necessary actions without court approval. (However, the less court approval necessary, the more vital it is either that the trustee have the minors' best interests at heart, or that other sources of supervision be available, perhaps in the form of an independent co-trustee.) A trust offers additional flexibility; it is not necessary that the trust property pass immediately to the minors as soon as they reach majority. It might reassure the testator or trustor if corpus is distributed in stages, say, 25% at majority, 50% at age 25, and the balance at age 30.

Where smaller amounts are involved, it may be better to use informal means: say, a bequest to an adult who understands that the property is to be transferred to a minor when he or she is mature enough to make use of it; a Totten trust or payable on death account with the minor as payee.

Several states have statutes dealing with small to medium-sized bequests to minors. California has adopted the Uniform Transfers to Minors Act (Probate §6341), expanding the Uniform Gifts to Minors Act to include trust-type transfers (for example, guardianships) as well as outright gifts. This Act has also been adopted by Colorado (§11-50-101) and Idaho (§68-801).

Under Delaware's Title 12 §2315, an executor or administrator who has control of a sum of money payable to an infant can deposit the money in a bank; get a certificate of deposit; and have the certificate recorded by the registrar of wills to evidence the propriety of the action.

In the District of Columbia (§20-1106), any sum payable to a minor can be paid over to the minor's guardian, if there is one; a direct distribution can be made, if the probate court approves. A sum under $1,000 can be deposited in a bank under a procedure similar to Delaware's or, with court approval, can be paid over to the minor's UGMA guardian.

Iowa's §633.108, dealing with dispositions under $4,000, permits the probate court to direct payment to the parent or guardian of a minor for whom no guardian has been appointed by the court. The direction requires an application by the executor or administrator.

Under New York's SCPA (Surrogate's Court Procedures Act) §2220, if an infant is a beneficiary of an estate, his or her share will be paid to the infant's guardian; if there is no guardian, it can be paid into court or deposited in a bank named by the court until the infant is 18 (the funds can be held longer if the court order so specifies). However, amounts under $5,000 can be paid or delivered to the infant's parent (or the adult with whom he or she lives) for the infant's use or benefit.

7

TRUST DRAFTING

A trust is a fiduciary relationship created by a *settlor* (also called *grantor* or *trustor*) who transfers property to a *trustee* so that the latter may administer it for the benefit of one or more *income beneficiaries*, and will eventually distribute the property to one or more *remaindermen*.

This is not the place for a comprehensive discussion of the ways in which trusts can be of use in an estate plan; I will merely point out that properly chosen and properly drafted trusts can:

- remove assets from the potentially taxable estate
- shift income to lower-bracket beneficiaries (within the limits imposed by tax law)
- avoid the need for conservatorship or guardianship by providing asset administration for an incompetent person

- manage the property of minors until they are ready to manage it for themselves
- centralize a person's property under professional management
- protect assets from the need to impoverish oneself to qualify for Medicaid, subject to the stringent provisions of the Comprehensive Omnibus Budget Reconciliation Act of 1985 (COBRA)
- simplify estate administration by uniting *inter vivos* trust assets and estate assets (via pourover).

However, it is impossible to achieve all these results simultaneously! Generally, the drafter must decide whether to pursue income and gift tax advantages or trade them off for estate planning advantages.

In order to have a valid trust, all these things must be present:

- a competent settlor
- a competent trustee, with provisions for succession if an original trustee becomes unwilling or unable to serve
- an identifiable trust *res* or *corpus* (although a trust can be set up with only nominal funding, with substantial funding to come later from insurance policies or a pourover from the estate)
- ascertainable beneficiary or beneficiaries
- limitations on the settlor's powers, so that the trust is more than the settlor's alter ego
- the intention to create a trust must be evident on the face of the trust instrument
- unless the Statute of Frauds can be avoided, there must, in fact, be a written instrument
- the trust's term must be set—and the trust must either terminate within the period specified by the Rule Against Perpetuities, or there must be a saving clause requiring termination in time
- the trust may be a "spendthrift" trust (which cannot be anticipated or alienated by the beneficiaries) but cannot be a fraudulent conveyance (used to defeat claims of the settlor's creditors, for example).

Although not strictly necessary for validity, a well-drafted trust instrument should also specify whether the trustee has the right to invade the trust corpus (give some of the trust's assets to one or more beneficiaries); under what circumstances invasion will be permitted; and whether the beneficiary's other assets should or must be considered before invading principal. ***PRACTICE TIP: In some states (New York, for example) a trust will be upheld if the trustee is directed not to invade principal for medical expenditures that would be covered by Medicaid; in other states (New Jersey is one), such a provision is considered invalid as against public policy. Another TIP: When drafting a trust, think seriously about including a provision permitting the trustee*** *to "apply income" for the benefit of a beneficiary, not just directing the beneficiary to "pay" the income to the beneficiary. If the beneficiary is incompetent, it may be necessary to appoint a guardian to receive the income.*

A well-drafted trust should include:

- a preamble, identifying the grantor and the basic type and purposes of the trust (family "sprinkle" trust; charitable remainder unitrust; Q-Tip trust, among others)

- identification of the trust property

- provision for later funding—either by direct contributions from the grantor, by payment of insurance policies, or by pourover from the grantor's will

- designation of original and successor trustees (TIP: make sure that the state permits out-of-state fiduciaries if any have been designated)

- fiduciary powers—in general, it is not necessary to spell out statutory powers, but it may be desirable to give the fiduciaries additional powers

- fiduciary compensation

- whether or not the fiduciary must be bonded

- identification of income beneficiaries and remaindermen. ***PRACTICE TIP:*** *If there is a class of beneficiaries, make sure that the treatment of illegitimate, adopted, and afterborn children is clear; make sure that the time as of which the class is determined is clear*

- treatment of income—is to be paid currently, or accumulated? May it be applied for the benefit of beneficiaries rather than paid directly to them? How should the income of infant beneficiaries be handled?

- if there are several beneficiaries, must they receive equal shares of income, or does the trustee have discretion to favor some over others?

- must the trustee favor the income beneficiaries over the remaindermen, or vice versa, or does the trustee have discretion?

- how should income and expenses be apportioned between income and principal of the trust?

- who, if anyone, has the power to amend, revoke, or modify the trust?

- can principal be invaded? If so, for whose benefit, on what standards, and who has discretion to make the choice? Can beneficiaries *demand* invasion of principal, and if so, in what amounts?

- what is the trust term? Is there a risk that the Rule Against Perpetuities might be violated; if so, is there a saving clause? Does the trustee have discretion to terminate the trust?

- if necessary for tax planning purposes, has the trustee's discretion been limited (has he or she been forbidden to purchase insurance policies on the grantor's life?)

- has provision been made for the possibility of beneficiaries dying in an order unanticipated by the grantor (for example, younger beneficiaries may predecease their elders)?
- may additions to corpus be made? If so, on what conditions?
- are there any spendthrift provisions? If so, are they valid under state law?
- speaking of that, which state's laws will govern the trust?

George Benton is 71; his wife, Mary Louise, is 67. Both are in good health, but are distressed by the experience relatives and friends have had with mentally and physically disabling conditions that are a part of the aging process. Therefore, each spouse has given the other spouse a durable power of attorney so he or she can handle business affiars for a spouse who is disabled (for instance, suffers a stroke or develops Alzheimer's Disease). Depending on the family situation, the amount and type of property they own, and the state they live in, establishment of one or more trusts could be a good planning alternative. For instance, a great deal of their property could be transferred to a family "sprinkle" trust with a legally independent yet sympathetic trustee who will provide income and principal as necessary. Such a trust could avoid the need for appointment of a guardian or conservator for Mr. or Mrs. Benton. However, the attorney must review current state and federal Medicaid regulations carefully to see what effect such a trust would have if the Bentons were to apply for Medicaid at a later time.

Once a first draft has been made of a trust, it must be edited very carefully with the tax laws in mind. Be very careful here—very small differences in wording, or the omission of a required provision, can result in the inclusion of trust corpus in the grantor's estate; can result in forfeiture of the marital deduction; or can result in loss of a charitable deduction. Particular attention must be paid to make sure that the trust qualifies for the gift-tax exemption, and that income beneficiaries have a "present interest" in the trust. The drafter must also be sure that, if the trust is in operation during the grantor's lifetime, that the "grantor trust" rules be circumvented; otherwise, the trust's income will be taxed to the grantor, and the income-shifting purpose will not be achieved.

Finally, the drafter must constantly review new tax law and proposed changes, and must notify clients of changes in tax law that make redrafting imperative.

Forms

SIMPLE WILL: Everything to Spouse;
Gift Over in Trust for Minor Children

a. I, _____, now living at _____ in the City of _____, State of _____, declare that this is my last will, and that by making this will I revoke all earlier wills and codicils.

b. If, at the time of my death, I am married to _____ and we have not been separated or divorced [and if he/she survives me by _____ days/months], I leave my entire estate to him/her.

c. If she/he does not survive me, or if we are separated or divorced at the time of my death, I leave my entire estate to my trustees, in trust.

d. "Entire estate" is defined as all the money, real estate, personal property, and powers of appointment located in any state, created by any document, and which I am entitled to dispose of by will.

e. I name my sister, _____, as executor of this will and trustee of the trust established by this will, and direct that she serve without bond or other security, and without compensation. If at any time she is unable or unwilling to serve in either of these capacities, I name the Trust Department of the _____ National Bank as executor and/or trustee, and direct that it receive the statutory commissions and post bond for its faithful performance.

f. I appoint my sister, _____, as guardian of the person and property of my children who are minors at the time of my death, if my spouse does not survive me [by 120 hours].

g. I direct that the trustee hold, manage, and invest the trust property until my youngest child reaches the age of 18/21.

h. During this time, the trustee will have discretion to sell trust property and reinvest the proceeds, and to expend, distribute, or accumulate trust income and/or principal for my children's personal, medical, and educational needs.

i. While my sister serves as trustee, she will have the statutory powers granted to a trustee, and will also have the power to borrow from the trust at market rates of interest, and to distribute trust income and/or principal to herself in reimbursement of personal funds advanced for my children's needs.

j. When my youngest child reaches 18/21, I direct that the trust be terminated, and an equal share of the remaining trust funds be distributed to each of my children surviving at that time.

COMMUNITY PROPERTY WILL
(Dispositive Provisions Only)

a. I own separate property as follows:

and direct that it be distributed as follows:

b. I am entitled to dispose of half the community property by will. My share of the community property may be described as follows:

and I direct that it be distributed as follows:

c. I am entitled to dispose of half the quasi-community property, as defined by §_____ of the statutes of the state of _____, by will. My share of the quasi-community property may be described as follows:

and I direct that it be distributed as follows:

SIMPLE WILL: All to Children if They Survive,
Otherwise to Spouse

NOTE: This will would typically be used for the younger and poorer spouse, who can be presumed to survive the older and richer spouse.

a. This is the last will of _____, a U.S. citizen living at _____. I hereby revoke all earlier wills and codicils.

b. Since _____, 19_____ I have been married to _____. [An earlier marriage to _____ ended with his/her death on _____, 19_____/ended in a divorce granted by the _____ Court of _____ on _____, 19_____.]

c. _____ children have been born of my current marriage: _____, born _____, 19_____; _____, born _____, 19_____; (etc.). (Recite children born to other marriages; adopted and step-children.)

d. I leave the sum of $_____ to my brother, _____.

e. I leave my diamond cocktail ring and my gold and ruby bracelet to my niece, _____.

f. I leave the entire rest and residue of my estate to such of my children who survive me, in equal shares. I direct my executor to divide the property into shares; his/her decision will be final.

If none of my children survives me, I leave the entire rest and residue to my spouse, _____; if I am survived neither by spouse nor by any children, to such of my brothers, sisters, nieces, and nephews who survive me, in equal shares.

g. I name my spouse, if he/she survives me, to serve as executor without bond and without compensation (other than reimbursement of expenses). If my spouse does not survive me, I name my brother, _____ as executor, under the same conditions.

h. I designate my sister, _____, and her husband, _____, as guardians of the person and property of any of my children who are minors at the time of my death, if my spouse does not survive me, or if he/she dies subsequent to my death without designating a guardian. No bond or security are to be required of the guardians.

SIMPLE WILL: Everything to Spouse;
Gift Over to Adult Children

NOTE: This will is based on an assumption that no more children will be born to, or adopted by, the testator and his/her spouse after execution of the will—the testator must be warned to revise his/her will and estate plan if more children are born or adopted.

a. This is the last will of _____, a citizen of the United States and of the state of _____. By making this will, I revoke all earlier wills and codicils.

b. I leave all my real and personal property of all types, wherever it is located, to my spouse, _____ [if he/she survives me by ____ days/if I am married and living with my spouse at the time of my death].

c. If my spouse does not survive [____ days] [or if we are separated or divorced at the time of my death] I leave all my real and personal property of all types, wherever it is located, to my children _____, _____, and _____ in equal shares. Valuation and decisions about the property and the mode of its distribution are in the sole discretion of my executor. If any of my children predeceases me, I direct the executor to distribute that child's share to his or her children in equal shares; if he/she has no surviving children, to the American Red Cross/the surviving children will divide my entire estate.

d. I appoint my spouse to serve as executor, without bond and without compensation other than reimbursement of expenses. If he/she does not survive me [by ____ days], or is unable to/unwilling to serve, I appoint my friend, _____, to serve as executor on the same terms. If he/she does not survive me, or is unable or unwilling to serve as executor, I appoint the _____ Bank and Trust Company as my executor.

SIMPLE WILL: SINGLE PERSON
Entire Estate to Person Rendering Services

a. This is the last will of _____, of _____. I hereby revoke all earlier wills and codicils.

b. I am not now married, and have never been married/my marriage to _____ ended on _____, 19_____ at his/her death/a divorce/annulment granted by the _____ Court of _____.

c. I have never had any children.

d. My intention is to leave my entire estate to _____, in return for the companionship and services he/she furnished as my business partner/as a homemaker/tending me during my illness and convalescence. If he/she does not survive me, I direct that my entire estate go to my friend _____/_____ University, my alma mater/my siblings who survive me, in equal shares.

e. My further intention is that no part of my estate go to my relatives or heirs at law by blood or by marriage (except if _____ does not survive me).

f. The decision to dispose of my property in this fashion is entirely my own, made after mature consideration and with advice of counsel. No person has coerced me or exercised undue influence to induce me to make this will.

g. I appoint my friend, _____, as executor of my will; if he/she is unable to serve, or refuses to serve, I appoint my friend, _____, as executor.

ABATEMENT

1. (General) If the estate is insufficient to pay debts, claims against the estate, administration expenses, and taxes, and still pay all legacies, I direct that abatement take place as follows:

2. (Dollar amount) If the net taxable estate (gross estate minus funeral expenses, expenses of administration, and debts) is less than $_____, I direct that abatement take place as follows:

3. (Measured by residue) If the residuary estate is less than $_____, I direct that abatement take place as follows:

4. (Money bequests abate) I direct that all bequests of personal property be made as provided by the will, but that all bequests of money shall abate; any funds not needed to satisfy claim against the estate will become part of the residuary estate.

5. (Priority order) I direct that specific bequests be paid in full in the order in which they appear in the will (that is, first the bequest made by Section ____, then by Section ____) until the available funds are exhausted. All other bequests will abate. Any sum of money remaining after the last bequest payable in full has been satisfied, but insufficient to pay the next bequest, will become part of the residue.

6. (Pro rata; cash) I direct the executor to sell all items specifically bequeathed within ____ months of my death, and to use the proceeds to satisfy the bequests on a pro rata basis.

7. (In full or not at all) I direct that the following bequests be paid in full: _____ and that all other bequests be revoked. Any funds so released will become part of the residue of my estate.

8. (In full or pro rata) I direct that the following bequests be paid in full: _____ and that all other bequests be paid in full: _____/and that all other bequests be paid pro rata from the remaining funds.

9. (By relationship) I direct that bequests to my spouse, children, siblings, nieces, nephews, and grandchildren be paid in full, and all other bequests be paid pro rata from any remaining funds.

OR

If the assets of my estate are not sufficient to pay all the legacies provided in this will in full, I direct that the assets be applied first to full payment of legacies to my spouse and children; next to full payment of legacies to other relatives; next to full payment of legacies to individuals other than my relatives; and, finally, to charitable legacies.

10. (Postscript to legacy) However, if my residuary estate is less than $_____, this gift will be reduced until it is no larger than ____% of the residuary estate.

OR

However, all legacies in this section are cancelled if the residuary estate is less than $_____. If the residuary estate is less than $_____ but more than $_____, the legacies will abate proportionately until they equal not more than ____% of my residuary estate.

11. (Charge on real estate) If my estate does not contain enough personal property to pay all the legacies in full, I direct my executor to sell as much real property as necessary, and to apply the proceeds to payment of the legacies.

ADEMPTION

1. (Lapse) If this item is not part of my estate at the time of my death, the gift will lapse.

2. (Comparable cash gift) If this item is not part of my estate at my death, I direct that the sum of $_____ be paid to him/her instead.

3. (Comparable item of property) If this item is not part of my estate at my death, I direct my executor to select a comparable item from my residuary estate and give it to the legatee. The executor's decision as to what constitutes a comparable item will be final.

OR

If there is no such item in my estate when I die, the legatee will have the right to select an item of comparable value from my residuary estate. If my executor believes the item so selected is of greater value than the item originally bequeathed, the executor will have full discretion to substitute another item or money from the residuary estate equal to the value of the adeemed item, for the item so chosen; or to receive from the legatee, in cash, the difference in value, which will become part of the residuary estate.

4. (Insurance proceeds) If ademption results from the loss, theft, or destruction of an insured item, occurring within ____ months before or ____ months after my death, the legatee will be entitled to any insurance proceeds payable to my estate.

ADVANCEMENTS

1. (Gifts are not advancements) I do not intend that any gifts made during my lifetime be treated as advancements.

2. (Post-will gifts are not advancements) No *inter vivos* gifts made by me after execution of this will are to be treated as advancements.

3. (Gifts are advancements if evidenced) I direct that any bequest of money be reduced by any advancement evidenced by a contemporary letter from me, or a contemporary acknowledgment from the donee, characterizing the transfer as an advancement.

OR

All advancements evidenced by contemporary writings, e.g., the following advancements:

Donee	Date	Amount or Description

and any others so evidenced after the making of this will and before my death, shall be subtracted from the bequests and residuary share due to the donee. No interest is to be charged on advancements, and valuation is to be made at an item of tangible property's appraised value for estate tax purposes. (If an item of tangible property is not part of the taxable estate, its valuation is to be made as if it were.)

4. (Class gifts in residuary estate) The following amounts have been received by the following beneficiaries:

Name	Date	Amount or Description

I direct that these amounts be added to the amount disposed of by this Section of my will (e.g., the residuary clause). I further direct that each person taking under this Section of my will receive an equal share of this augmented amount, minus anything he/she has already received as an advancement. Tangible property shall be valued according to appraisals made because or as if the property were part of the taxable estate.

CROSS-REFERENCE: See RELATED WRITINGS.

ADVANCEMENTS

1. Letter contemporaneous with gift

Dear _____,
I am now making you a gift of $_____/the following item:

This money/property is a final and absolute gift to you. However, I consider it an advancement—that is, it will reduce your share of my estate.

Signed: Date:

OR

Dear _____,
Here is your (description) _____. It is an advancement in partial/total satisfaction of your interest as a beneficiary under my will/a distributee of my estate. The value of the advancement is $_____, as evidenced by:

Signed: Date:

2. Acknowledgment of advancement

Dear _____,
On _____, 19____, I received your gift of $_____/item(s) described as follows:

I acknowledge that this absolute gift will be treated as an advancement— that is, it has been taken into account in drafting bequests, and will reduce any percentage share of your estate to which I become entitled.

Signed: Date of acknowledgment:

AFTERBORN CHILDREN

NOTE: The need for such a clause can be eliminated by phrasing gifts to children in terms of "to each of my children surviving me" rather than dispositions to named children. However, if it is unlikely but not impossible that the testator and his/her spouse (whether the spouse at the time of execution of the will or at the time of the testator's death) will bear or adopt more children, a clause dealing with afterborn children should be included in the will.

1. (Equality) My intention is that children born to me and my spouse, or adopted by me and my spouse, after the date of execution of this will, be treated equally in all respects with their siblings born or adopted before execution of this will.

NOTE: This clause is suitable for use with a provision distributing the residuary estate and/or trust principal "to my children in equal shares."

2. (Equality; reduces residuary estate) If any children are born to my spouse and myself, or adopted by us, after execution of this will, my intention is that the residuary estate be reduced so that each afterborn child receives a monetary legacy equal to that provided for my children now living.

NOTE: This clause is suitable where the residuary legatee is someone other than the children—e.g., the spouse; a friend; a charity. It is probably best avoided where the provision for the afterborns would reduce the surviving spouse's inheritance.

3. (No provision for afterborns) My intention is that any children born to me or adopted by me after execution of this will shall not receive any specific legacy or share of my residuary estate, because I know that my spouse will provide for their financial needs and well-being out of his/her own financial resources and the provision I have made for him/her in this will.

CROSS-REFERENCE: See DISINHERITANCE.

APPORTIONMENT OF ESTATE TAX

1. (No apportionment) I direct that all estate and inheritance taxes imposed on my estate be paid out of my residuary estate, as an expense of administration, and shall not be apportioned among my legatees.

2. (Apportionment only as to taxable non-probate property) The proportion of estate tax on my estate traceable to property passing by will is to be paid from my residuary estate without apportionment. I direct my executor to pay any and all taxes traceable to the assets of my *inter vivos* trust, created on _____, 19_____, according to the terms of that trust, which are hereby incorporated by reference. Any taxes traceable to property forming part of my taxable estate but neither subject to probate administration nor part of the assets of my *inter vivos* trust are to be paid by my executor. I direct that my executor charge such taxes against the non-probate property, and obtain reimbursement from the inheritors of such property.

3. (Full apportionment) I direct that every devise, legacy, and residuary legacy be reduced by a proportionate share of any estate and/or inheritance tax due on my estate.

4. (Exoneration of immediate family) I direct that any estate or inheritance tax due on my estate be paid by the beneficiaries except for my surviving spouse and children. Taxes will be charged against each beneficiary according to his/her share of the portion of the total estate other than that bequeathed to my spouse and children.

OR

Although my executor is responsible in the first instance for payment of estate and inheritance taxes and corresponding interest and penalties, I direct that the ultimate payors be those who inherit my taxable estate (whether probate or non-probate property). However, I exonerate my spouse/my spouse and children/my residuary legatee from payment of such taxes.

I direct my executor to apportion the taxes among my other heirs, according to the proportion of my taxable estate, other than portions of my taxable estate passing to exonerated parties, that they receive. I further direct my executor to withhold the appropriate amount from any property distributable to a non-exonerated heir, and to take any other action required to collect the estate and inheritance taxes from those ultimately responsible for their payment.

5. (Power of appointment) If any property is included in my gross estate because I had a general power of appointment over the property, and if this inclusion results in the imposition of any federal or state estate tax and/or state inheritance tax, I direct that such taxes be allocated to the appointive property and paid by the recipient of the property (including the trustee, if such property is payable to a trust).

6. (Q-Tip) I am the income beneficiary of Q-Tip property under Section
_____ of the will of my spouse, _____, who died on
_____, 19____. This property is includible in my gross taxable
estate under Code §____. If inclusion results in the imposition of federal
estate tax, I direct that the tax be apportioned as follows:

7. (Insurance proceeds) If any insurance on my life is includible in my
gross estate, is payable to any beneficiary other than my spouse, and if
this inclusion results in the imposition of federal or state estate tax and/or
state inheritance tax. I direct that the tax liability be allocated to the
insurance proceeds and paid by the beneficiary. If the proceeds are
payable to my spouse, I direct my executor to pay any such tax liability **as**
an expense of administration.

8. (Insufficient estate) If the residuary estate is too small to pay the taxes
with which it is charged, I direct that payment be made as follows:

CROSS REFERENCE: See ABATEMENT.

ATTESTATION

1. (Long form) on _____, 19____, a person whom we knew to be
_____ showed us a ____-page document and told us it was
his/her will. He/she signed at the end of the will [and at the end of each
page]. He/she showed us where he/she had signed the will. All the
witnesses were present when he/she told us this.

   We hereby sign_____'s will as witnesses, at his/her
request; all the witnesses are present and in the presence of the testator
at the signing.

Date
Name   Address   Signature

2. (Testator's competency) to the best of our knowledge and belief, the
testator was of sound mind, understood the nature of his/her property
and the effects of signing the will, and was not induced to sign the will by
anyone's fraud, menace, duress, or undue influence.

3. (Codicil) On _____, 19____, a person whom we knew to be
_____ showed us a ____-page document and told us it was
the _____ Codicil to his/her will dated _____, 19____.
(Continue as above).

CODICILS

1. (General form) With reference to Section _____ of my will dated
_____, 19_____, I hereby direct as follows:
In all other respects, I confirm and republish that will.

OR

As a first (or second, etc.) codicil to my will dated _____, 19_____, I
reaffirm and republish the will and all earlier codicils, except as follows:

2. (Additional bequest) I bequeath the sum of $_____ to
_____, in addition to any other provision for him/her made
in my will.

OR

I bequeath (item of personal property) to _____. If this item
is not in my possession at my death, the gift will lapse/I direct that my
executor select a comparable item from my residuary estate and give it to
_____/I direct that my executor pay _____ the
sum of $_____ from my residuary estate.

3. (Revocation of bequest) I hereby revoke the bequest of $_____/
item of personal property: _____ made to
_____ by Section _____ of my will. Instead, I direct that this
sum/item become part of my residuary estate/be given to
_____.

4. (Revocation of appointment) I revoke the appointment of
_____ as executor/trustee/guardian. Instead, I nominate and
appoint _____ as executor/trustee/guardian, to serve with/
without bond.

CROSS-REFERENCE: See EXECUTORS (Compensation).

5. (Revocation of codicil) I revoke the First (Second, etc.) codicil, and
substitute the following provision for the provisions of the revoked codicil:

DEFINITIONS

1. (Just debts) I direct my executor to pay all my just debts, including the
$_____ I owe to _____, which is unenforceable
because the statute of limitations has expired/because I was charged in
bankruptcy by order #_____ of the _____ Court,
dated _____, 19_____.

OR

"Just debts" includes any arrears of alimony or child support I owed at
the time of my death.

CROSS-REFERENCE: See RELEASE OF DEBTS.

2. (Per capita) If property or a sum of money is to be divided "per capita,"
it means that the material to be divided is divided into shares of equal
value, with one share going to each person benefited, regardless of their
ages or their relationship to me.

3. (Per stirpes) If property or a sum of money is to be divided "per
stirpes," it means that the material to be divided into shares of equal
value, one each for each of the children born to me. If any of my children
dies before I do, his or her share is to be further divided equally among
his or her children.

4. (Plural beneficiaries) In any disposition of an item of property or
collection of items of property to several people, I intend that they take as
joint tenants/as tenants in common.

5. (Real property) "Real property" means land and estates in land,
including leaseholds, fixtures, and mortgages; including ownership
interests in condominiums, but not in cooperative apartments.

6. (Tactful provision for illegitimate child) Any reference in my will to
"children" or "issue" includes _____, born _____,
19_____ and whose mother/father is _____.

DISCLAIMERS

1. (By antenuptial agreement) I, _____, contemplate marriage to _____. Each of us has made full disclosure of our financial assets, liabilities, and obligations, and each of us has gotten the advice of an attorney. After consideration of our financial situation and that of our spouses-to-be, each of us has decided to waive any right of election or right to an intestate share of the property of the other. Each of us agrees to accept whatever provision the other makes for him/her in her/his will, and agrees not to institute a will contest.

CROSS-REFERENCE: See DISINHERITANCE.

2. (By separation agreement) Whether or not a divorce is granted, and unless we reconcile and resume living together as spouses, each of us agrees to renounce any bequest, devise, legacy, elective share, or intestate share in the estate of the other.

NOTE: State statutes typically refer to revocation of provisions in favor of the ex-spouse on divorce, not separation. To disinherit the estranged spouse, a separation agreement must show an explicit intent to disinherit (or renounce) and must be completely inconsistent with any will. See, e.g., Estate of Beauchamp, 115 AZ 219, 564 P2d 908 (1977); In re Maruccia, 54 NY2d 196, 445 NYS2d 73 (1981).

DISINHERITANCE

1. (Personal reasons) For personal reasons known to him/her, I make no provision for my (relationship) _____, _____ or his/her issue. He/she and his/her issue are not to receive any legacy or intestate share of my estate, and I direct that my property be disposed of as if he/she had predeceased me.

2. (Advancements) I have not left any money or property to _____, believing that he/she has already received a fair share of my estate in the form of gifts made during my lifetime.

3. (Assets needed elsewhere) I do not make any monetary provision for my (relationship) _____ _____, not because of any animosity between us, but because I feel that the assets of my estate can be more appropriately applied elsewhere.

4. (Omission of children not accidental) No provision has been made for my children, now living or afterborn, because I believe that my spouse, _____, will care for them and make appropriate financial provision for them.

OR

No provision has been made by will for my children, now living or afterborn, because I have created an *inter vivos* trust/testamentary trust which I believe is adequate for their financial needs.
NOTE: Either of these clauses should remove the will from the reach of state pretermission statutes, which refer to possibly unintentional omission of natural heirs.
CROSS-REFERENCE: See AFTERBORN CHILDREN.

5. (Spouse—pursuant to antenuptial contract) No provision for my spouse, _____, has been made by this will. The omission is intentional, and does not stem from anger or lack of affection. My spouse and I executed an antenuptial contract on _____, 19____ in contemplation of our marriage, renouncing all testamentary, intestate, or elective share in the estate of the other. This contract was motivated by a desire to maintain our financial affairs separately, to benefit our families and other natural objects of our bounty, and to minimize our tax obligations through legitimate use of planning devices.
CROSS-REFERENCE: See DISCLAIMERS.

6. I do not intend to benefit any other person under my will. However, to prevent challenges to my will and estate plan, I leave $1 to any person who demonstrates that he/she is my heir to the satisfaction of any court having jurisdiction over my estate.

NOTE: The purpose of this clause is to integrate disinheritance and in terrorem clauses. See, for example, Matter of Hilton, 98 NM 420, 649 P2d 488 (1982).

DISPOSITIVE PROVISIONS

A. CLASSIFIED BY RECIPIENT

1. (To spouse—minimum elective share) I direct my executor to distribute to my spouse, _____, if he/she survives me [by ____ days] such money and property which will, when added to other money and property passing to him/her outside the will, equal the minimum elective share provided by the laws of the state of _____. The executor's choice of funding mechanisms will be final.

2. (To spouse—maximum marital pecuniary disposition) If my spouse, _____, survives me [by ____ days], I give him/her the smallest dollar amount that will reduce my taxable estate so that the estate tax (after all allowable credits) will be zero. However, this bequest will not be satisfied by transferring to my spouse any property or the proceeds of any property not qualifying for the federal estate tax marital deduction.

3. (To spouse—fractional marital bequest) If my spouse, _____, survives me [by ____ days], I leave him/her a fraction of my residuary estate represented by x/y, where x equals the amount necessary to be used as an estate tax marital deduction to reduce the federal estate tax, computed after all allowable credits, to zero. Y equals the aggregate value of my residuary estate. Valuation is computed as finally determined in the federal estate tax proceedings relative to my estate, but without provision for estate or inheritance taxes, interest, or penalties.

All property and proceeds transferred to my spouse in satisfaction of this disposition must be eligible for the federal estate tax marital deduction.

4. (Pecuniary equalization disposition) I leave to my spouse, _____, if he/she survives me [by ____ days], the minimum amount necessary to make our taxable estates equal, given the assumption that my spouse dies immediately after I do. No property or proceeds not qualifying for the federal estate tax marital deduction may be transferred to my spouse in satisfaction of this disposition.

5. (Short form) If my spouse, _____, survives me [by ____ days], I give him/her $_____ minus all other non-testamentary property or property interests qualifying for the federal estate tax marital deduction. However, I direct that my executor satisfy this disposition only by transferring to my spouse property qualifying for the federal estate tax marital deduction.

CROSS-REFERENCE: See INSURANCE PROCEEDS.

6. (Bequest to cohabitant) I give and bequeath my entire estate/____% of my estate/the entire rest and residue of my estate to _____, with whom I have been cohabiting since _____, 19____.

   With regard to identification of property as joint property, my individual property subject to this will, and _____'s individual property belonging to him/her alone, a cohabitation agreement between _____ and myself, dated _____, 19____ and as amended, is hereby incorporated by reference, and shall be final and determinative.

7. (Gift to minor—guardian) Any bequest to a person who is under 18/21 at the time the bequest is payable, shall be paid or distributed to the minor's parent or guardian, for the use and benefit of the minor.

8. (Gift to minor—UGMA custodian) Any money or property payable to a minor, under this will or a testamentary trust created under this will, shall vest absolutely in the minor. However, the executor(s) and/or trustee(s) are directed to/have the discretion to distribute the property to the minor's mother/the minor's father/to _____/to him- or herself/to the person designated as the minor's custodian, to act as custodian for the minor's property under the Uniform Gifts to Minors Act. [Such property is to be retained by the custodian until the minor reaches the age of 21].

9. (Gift to minor—deposit in specified bank) Any pecuniary legacy less than $_____ and payable to a minor for whom a guardian of the property has not been appointed, is to be deposited into the _____ Bank, subject to the supervision of the _____ Court.

NOTE: See, for example, New York SCPA §2220(3).

10. (Power in trust) I leave my coin collection to my nephew, _____. If he is a minor at the time of my death, I give his mother, my sister, _____, a power in trust to hold the coin collection for him, and turn it over to him when he reaches 21.

OR

If any devisee or legatee is under 21/18 when the devise or legacy is payable or distributable, the money or property is to be distributed to _____ as the donee of a power during minority. _____ is charged with protecting and managing such property until its minor owner reaches majority.

11. (Class gift) I give the amount of $_____ to each of my issue who survives me. "Issue" means my children (born to me and adopted by me including/excluding step-children) and their children, defined in the same way.

OR

I give the amount of $_____ to each of my children and step-children/including adopted children but excluding step-children. If any of my children predeceases me but is survived by children (as defined above), his or her children who survive me will divide the share of their deceased parent equally.

OR

To my grandchildren _____ and _____ I give $_____ each to be paid when each reaches the age of 15. I give the same amount to any grandchildren born after the execution of this will, payable to each when he/she reaches the age of 15.

12. (Bequests conditional on behavior) I bequeath the sum of $_____ to my son-in-law/daughter-in-law, _____, on condition that he/she is living with my son/daughter, _____, or is his/her surviving spouse at the time of my death. If they have separated or divorced before my death this sum is to become part of my residuary estate/be paid to the children of my son/daughter, _____, alive at the time of my death, in equal shares.

OR

This bequest is made on condition that he/she lives with her parents until reaching the age of 21/graduates from college on or before _____, 19____/refrains from marrying outside his/her religion/ _____. If this condition is not met, the bequest is void, and the money becomes part of my residuary estate.

13. (Employee) I give the sum of $_____ each to _____ and _____ if they are still working for me at the time of my death.

OR

I give the sum of $_____ to every employee of _____ Corp. who is employed at the time of my death, and who has more than _____ years of service with the company.

14. (Charitable bequest—short form) I give to _____ or its successor the smaller of the sum of $_____ or _____% of my distributable estate.

OR

I give the sum of $_____ to _____, organized as a charitable corporation under the laws of the state of _____, or to its successor. This amount is to be used exclusively for charitable or educational purposes.

OR

I leave the sum of $_____ to the charitable organization known as _____ or its successor. However, if this organization or its successor is not a "charity" as defined by Section 2055 of the Internal Revenue Code, I direct that this legacy be paid to the American Red Cross/ become part of my residuary estate/be paid to _____or his/her estate.

15. (Charitable bequest—executor selects charity) I give $_____ to a charitable organization to be chosen by my executor, bearing in mind my interest in the performing arts/cancer research/Zionism/education for the blind/propagation of the Gospel. I direct my executor to restrict his/her choice of charitable organizations to those defined as "charities" by §2055 of the Internal Revenue Code.

16. (Charitable bequest—items—conditional) I bequeath my collection of eighteenth-century porcelain and silver to the _____
Museum, on condition that, at all times, it either be exhibited in the public galleries or preserved for the examination of art students and scholars. Any piece, or the entire collection, shall revert to my sister, _____, or her estate if at any time it ceases to be so exhibited or preserved.

OR

I bequeath the full-length oil portraits of my father, grandfather, and great-grandfather to the East Overshoe Historical Society on condition that they hang the portraits and maintain them on public display at the Historical Society offices. If at any time the portraits are removed from public display, I direct that this bequest be divested, and that the portraits become the absolute property of my niece, _____, or her estate.

NOTE: These provisions are designed to protect the property from "de-acquisition" by the beneficiary—that is, sale for its own benefit. But before including such a provision, it makes sense to find out if the recipient wants the item in the first place. They may refuse, or may insist that funds be provided for upkeep.

CROSS-REFERENCE: See CHARITABLE REMAINDER ANNUITY TRUST, and CHARITABLE REMAINDER UNITRUST.

B. CLASSIFIED BY TYPE OF PROPERTY

1. (Demonstrative disposition) I give to _____ the sum of $_____, to be paid out of my account(s) with _____ Bank existing at the time of my death.

OR

I give to _____ the amount of $_____, to be paid out of the proceeds of the sale of my house/yacht/art collection, etc.

OR

To _____, who now lives at _____, I give the sum of $_____, payable from my account #_____ at the _____ Branch of the _____ Bank. However, if at the time of my death, this account is insufficient, I direct that the legacy be paid out of this account to the extent possible, with the balance of the legacy coming from the general assets of the estate.

OR

To my friend, _____, if he/she survives me [by 60 days], I leave the sum of $_____ to be paid from Account #_____ in the _____ Bank; or all the funds in the account at the time of my death, whichever is less.

2. (Fractional bequest) My "net testamentary estate" equals my gross testamentary estate minus debts and the expenses of my funeral and the administration of my estate. I bequeath _____% of my net estate to _____; _____% to _____; _____% to _____. If any of them does not survive me, his/her bequest becomes part of my residuary estate/passes to his/her surviving spouse/ passes to his/her children in equal shares/passes to his/her issue *per stirpes.*

3. (Real estate—devise of residence in sole name) To my spouse, _____, I devise the house at _____, or any principal residence solely owned by me and in which we are residing at the time of my death.

4. (Real estate—devise of residence; mortgage insurance) I direct that my executor satisfy, from the assets of my residuary estate, any encumbrance on my principal residence, so that it passes free and clear. However, I advise my executor that the mortgage on my principal residence is now covered by a mortgage insurance policy #_____ issued by the _____ Company, and direct my executor to exhaust the proceeds of that policy (or any successor policy owned by me at the time of my death) before using the assets of my residuary estate.

5. (Life estate—Q-tip property) a. To my spouse, _____, if he/ she survives me [by _____ days] I devise/bequeath a life estate in the following property:

b. If he/she does not so survive me, I devise/bequeath such property to _____ absolutely.

c. Such property is to pass to my spouse without requiring him/her to give any security for it.

d. With respect to such property, my spouse will have all the powers granted to my executor by Section _____ of this will.

e. When my spouse dies, the property is to be distributed to _____/is to be distributed as he/she shall appoint by will; or, if he/she shall make no such appointment, to _____. My spouse's executor or administrator is hereby given the power to take possession of the property in order to transfer it to its rightful owner(s), and may, if it is deemed necessary or desirable, sell part or all of the property and distribute its proceeds.

f. I direct my executor/my executor has discretion as to part or all of the property to treat the disposition as one of Qualified Terminable Interest Property.

g. Receipts and payments with respect to this property are to be allocated between income and principal as provided by the laws of the state of _____.

6. (Life estate—gift over) To my son, _____, if he survives me, I give the use of the house located at _____ for the term of his life. He will be responsible for real estate taxes and the expenses of

maintaining the house in habitable condition and preventing waste. At his death, I give the property to the oldest of his children then surviving. If he is not survived by children, I give the property to my oldest grandchild surviving at the time of my son's death.

OR

...However, the carrying costs of such property (including but not limited to real estate taxes, repairs, insurance, and mortgage payments) are to be paid by my executor out of my residuary estate.

7. (Condominium) To _____ (or to _____ if _____ does not survive me) I devise my condominium unit #_____ located at _____, and any insurance policies covering the condominium unit, subject to/free from any mortgage against this condominium unit existing at the time of my death.

8. (Co-op) To _____ (or to _____, if _____ does not survive me) I give the proprietary lease and all my _____ shares of stock in the _____ Cooperative Corporation evidencing my rights in Apartment #_____ located at _____. He/she will be responsible for payment of maintenance and periodic assessments.

9. (Insurance) If, at the time I die, I am the owner or insured of any life insurance policies payable to my estate, I give the proceeds of such policies to _____.

OR

I give the first $_____ of proceeds of insurance policies on my life and payable to my estate to _____; I give any remaining proceeds to _____.

OR

I direct that the proceeds of any policies of life insurance on my life payable to my estate, become part of my residuary estate.

OR

All proceeds of insurance policies payable to my estate on account of my death are to be distributed to the testamentary trust established by Section _____ of this will.

OR

I direct that any proceeds of insurance on my life and payable to my estate be poured over into the *inter vivos* trust I created on _____, 19_____ and be administered under the terms of that trust, which are hereby incorporated by reference.

OR

With regard to insurance proceeds on my life payable to my estate, I direct that such proceeds be paid to my spouse, _____, if he/she survives me, in _____ installments, with the first installment to be paid not more than 13 months after my death. I further direct that my spouse have the power to appoint such proceeds by deed or by will.

OR

The proceeds of Policy #_____, issued by the _____ Co. on my life, are payable to my estate. I direct that the insurer hold these proceeds in trust for my spouse, _____, if he/she survives me, pay interest on such proceeds at least annually, and pay out such proceeds as my spouse shall appoint by will or by deed.

NOTE: See Code §2056(b)(2).

10. (Closely held business) I bequeath all my shares in _____, a closely held corporation, to _____.

NOTE: Is there a voting agreement, voting trust, or buy-sell agreement controlling the disposition of the shares, or giving a right of first refusal to the entity or the other stockholders?

OR

My shares in _____ Corp., a closely held business, are covered by a buy-sell agreement/voting trust/voting agreement/transfer restrictions dated _____, 19____, made between me and _____. The provisions of this document are hereby incorporated by reference. As a result of this document, the corporation/ my fellow shareholders have a right of first refusal over my shares. If they exercise this right, I direct that the consideration paid for my shares be paid to my spouse if he/she survives me by 120 hours/50% to my spouse, 50% to my children _____ and _____ in equal shares/become part of my residuary estate/be paid to the trustee of the testamentary trust established by this will/be paid to the trustee of an *inter vivos* trust I established on _____, 19____.

11. (Accounts receivable) I give all accounts receivable of the business known as _____, which I operated at _____, to _____. My executor shall have absolute discretion to arrange payment schedules and compromise payment of otherwise uncollectable accounts receivable, and will not be accountable to the estate for losses or uncollectable accounts receivable.

12. (Patent) I bequeath my entire interest in U.S. Patent No. _____, issued _____, 19____ covering the following subject matter: _____ to _____.

13. (Copyright) To _____, I give all my rights to exploit a book/film/painting/etc. known as _____, for the period of fifty years after my death. I direct my executor to see that registration of this transfer is made pursuant to 17 USCA §205.

14. (Personal papers) I bequeath all my personal papers to _____. This bequest includes all correspondence, diaries, unpublished manuscripts, and holographic and interim versions of

published works, but does not include legal documents such as contracts, deeds, and mortgages.

15. (Bequest for masses) To the pastor of the Church of _____, located at _____, I give the sum of $_____ and request that he say masses for the repose of my soul/ the soul of _____.

16. (Exercise of power of appointment) I was given a power of appointment under Section ____ of the will of _____. _____ died on _____, 19____; his/her will was admitted to probate on _____, 19____ by the _____ Court of _____, under file number _____. I now exercise the power of appointment and direct that the appointive property be distributed as follows: _____

17. (Disclaimed property) All property subject to a valid disclaimer will be divided in equal shares among the takers of my residuary estate, with the exception of the person making the disclaimer.

18. (Pourover) On _____, 19____, I created an *inter vivos* called the _____ Trust. I direct that the following property be paid to the trust on my death: _____. The property so contributed and the *inter vivos* trust shall form a single trust administered under the terms of the *inter vivos* trust. I do not intend to create a separate testamentary trust, nor do I intend to bring the *inter vivos* trust within the jurisdiction of the probate court.

19. (Pourover to someone else's trust) If my spouse, _____ survives me, I give the sum of $_____/the entire residue of my estate to the trustees of an *inter vivos* trust created by my spouse on _____, 19____, to become part of the principal of that *inter vivos* trust, administered under its terms.

20. (Revocation of Totten trust) My savings account #_____ at the _____ Branch of the _____ Bank, located at _____, is in the form of a Totten trust with _____ as beneficiary. I hereby revoke that Totten trust, and direct that any amount in that account at the time of my death be paid to _____, instead.

21. (Contents) To _____, I give and bequeath whatever is contained within Safety Deposit Box #_____, at the _____ Branch of the _____ Bank, located at _____.

OR

I give the entire contents of my house as of the time of my death, to _____.

OR

I leave the contents of my residence to _____; however, this bequest does not include any cash, checks, securities, or evidences of indebtedness within my residence at the time of my death.

22. (Bulk bequests of personal property) I leave all tangible personal property (except cash), not disposed of elsewhere in this will, and which is in my possession at the time of my death, to my spouse, _____, if he/she survives me.

If he/she does not survive me, I leave this tangible personal property to my children who survive me. The respective shares of each child, and the property to be distributed in each share, are to be determined by agreement of my adult children and the guardians of my minor children. If they cannot agree, the property will be divided by my executor, taking the personal preferences of my children into account. However, the decision of my executor will be final and binding on everyone with an interest in my estate.

OR

I bequeath all my tangible personal property other than cash to _____ as an individual and not in his/her capacity as executor, in the hope that he/she will distribute it as I would wish, and in accordance with the wishes of my family and friends. However, this bequest is outright, unconditional, and does not create a trust.

OR

Each of the following people, in this order, will have the right to select up to three items from my residuary estate:
1.
2.
3. (etc.)

OR

I give the following people a right of selection among my personal property (other than precious jewelry and articles otherwise bequeathed by earlier provisions of this will): 1. _____ 2. _____ 3. _____ (etc.) If any of them predecease me, the survivors of this group will have the right of selection.

The first person so named may select one article of his/her choice; next, _____ may choose one article, and so forth. They may continue making choices in this manner as long as they wish, until my tangible personal property is exhausted/until each has received ____ articles.

OR

Except for items already bequeathed by earlier provisions of this will, I bequeath to my spouse, if he/she survives me, the following:

• all my clothing
• all the household furniture and furnishings of my residence at the time of my death
• all television sets, computers, stereos, and other electronic equipment

- all artwork and decorative objects
- insurance proceeds traceable to the loss, theft, or destruction of any of the above within _____ months before my death or during the period of administration of my estate.

If my spouse does not survive me, I bequeath the objects described above to my children who survive me, in equal shares. Division of these items will be done by the executor, whose decision will be final.

23. (Residuary clauses) I devise, give, and bequeath all the rest of my property (real, personal, and mixed) which can be transmitted by will, to _____. This gift includes property over which I have a power of appointment and dispositions made earlier in this will which have lapsed.

OR

I direct my executor to divide the residue of my estate into two equal portions. "Residue" is defined as all real, personal, or mixed property which I owned, had an interest in, or had a power of appointment over at the time of my death.

If my spouse, _____, survives me, one share goes to her, the other share to my surviving children, to be divided in equal shares among them. If my spouse does not survive me, the residue is to be divided equally among my children who survive me.

OR

I direct that the residue of my estate be divided equally between my children, _____ and _____; provided, however, that _____ is to receive all my jewelry and _____ is to receive all the power tools from my workshop.

OR

The residue of my estate is to be divided into equal shares, one for each of my children (including/excluding illegitimate, adopted, and step-children). If any of my children predeceases me, his or her share is to be divided equally among any children of his or hers who survive me. If any of my children predeceases me and is not survived by any legitimate children, his or her share is to be divided equally among my children who survive me.

OR

I give, bequeath, and devise my residuary estate to my trustee, in trust. I direct the trustee to manage and invest the residuary estate, and pay the income at least quarterly to _____ during his/her life.

If and when _____ appoints the property during his/her lifetime or by will, I direct the trustee to transfer as much of the principal as has been appointed by _____, to the person(s) or entity(ies) named by _____. The power of appointment may be exercised in _____'s own favor, in favor of his/her creditors, and in favor of his/her estate and its creditors.

24. (Anti-lapse for residuary clause) If any residuary beneficiary dies before I do, his/her share of the residue is to be divided among the other residuary beneficiaries in the same proportion their legacies bore to the residue as a whole. That is, a beneficiary receiving 25% of the original residue would receive 25% of the residuary share of the predeceased residuary beneficiary, and so on.

C. ADMINISTRATION OF DISPOSITIVE PROVISIONS

1. (Reduction to cash) I direct that my executor sell my house located at _____ with/without the services of a broker, as soon as possible consistent with receiving the highest price reasonably obtainable. Sales proceeds will become part of my residuary estate.

OR

I direct that my entire estate be reduced to cash, in order to pay all debts, charges against my estate, bequests, devises, and legacies in cash form.

In order to do this, I instruct my executor to sell and convey all real estate on terms and security in his discretion, and to sell all personal property by public or private sale (at the executor's discretion). Neither court order nor appraisal shall be required. Private sales may take place without notice; notice for public sales shall be as my executor determines, in his sole discretion.

2. (No interest) No interest is to be paid on any bequest or devise under this will. As for real or personal property constituting my residuary estate, any income accruing to such assets during the period of administration shall become part of my estate in general, and the estate in general is chargeable with the expenses of maintaining this property.

3. (Shipping charges) I direct that my executor pay all charges of packing, shipping, and insuring such property while it is in transit to the beneficiary, and that these charges be treated as an expense of administration.

OR

Beneficiaries of specific bequests of personal property shall be responsible for either picking up the items of property left to them, or for arranging transportation, packing, and insurance at their own expense.

4. (Accelerated Delivery) To _____, I leave the amount of $_____/the following item(s): _____ _____ with payment or delivery to be made within thirty days of the time my executor(s) has/have been granted letters testamentary.

5. (Delayed Distribution) A large portion of my estate consists of illiquid assets, e.g., _____. Therefore, I authorize my executor to delay distribution of legacies for a period of up to ____ years after my death if, in my executor's discretion, this delay would make it possible to obtain a higher price for these illiquid assets. I exonerate the executor of all claims based on such a delay undertaken in good faith. No interest will be payable to the beneficiaries as a result of the delay in distribution.

ELECTIVE SHARE

CROSS-REFERENCE: See DISCLAIMERS.

1. (Spouse's election to take under will in lieu of elective share—attachment to will) I, _____ am the wife/husband of _____, the testator of the will to which this statement is attached. After careful consideration of the terms of the will, and after advice of counsel about my legal rights, I hereby accept the provisions of the will as they apply to me, and hereby waive all right of election and right of dower/courtesy.

      Therefore, I have signed this statement in the presence of _____ witnesses, on _____, 19_____, at _____ in the City of _____, County of _____, and State of _____. (Signature and acknowledgment).

2. (Unilateral waiver of right of election—specified property) a. _____ and _____ intend to marry on _____, 19_____. If this marriage takes place, and if _____ is the surviving spouse at the time of _____'s death, he/she agrees to waive all rights of election and right to receive a distributive share of _____'s property.

b. In return for this renunciation, _____ agrees to make a fair provision for _____ by maintaining at all times a valid will providing at least the following: an absolute disposition of _____ to him/her, plus a life estate in _____.

c. The executor of the will of the spouse making such provision will have discretion to treat property so passing as "qualified terminable interest property" to the extent permitted by law.

Date: Signatures:

ENCUMBRANCES

NOTE: State laws usually provide that, in the absence of a will provision to the contrary, encumbered property passes subject to the encumbrance.

1. (Full exoneration) As to all encumbered property in my estate/as to the following encumbered property: I direct my executor to satisfy all encumbrances in full from the assets of the residuary estate, so that all property passed by this will passes free and clear.

2. (Joint property) If any joint property owned by me and my spouse is subject to any mortgage, lien, or security interest at the time of my death, I direct my executor to satisfy the encumbrance from the assets of my residuary estate.

NOTE: Reg. §20.2056(b)-4(b) says that the value of property passing to a surviving spouse is reduced by any encumbrance, for valuation of the estate tax marital deduction. However, if the terms of the will or local law call for exoneration or reimbursement of the encumbrance, the amount involved is an additional interest passing to the surviving spouse.

EXECUTORS: APPOINTMENT

1. (Single executor/person) I name _____, my
_____, as executor of my will [and trustee of the trust
created by this will]. He/she is to serve without bond and without
compensation.

2. (Single executor/institution) I appoint the _____ Bank and
Trust Company of _____ as executor of my will [and trustee
of the trust created by this will], to serve without bond.

3. (Appointment of successor) If at any time a person named as executor
and/or trustee becomes unable or unwilling to continue serving as
fiduciary, he/she may appoint a successor [using these criteria:] provided,
however, that he/she not resign as fiduciary without appointing a
successor and having him/her qualify. However, I require that the
successor fiduciary give a bond to secure faithful performance, whether
or not the original fiduciary gave bond.

4. (Named person to choose) I give my spouse/son/daughter the power to
choose an executor from this list:

Name   *Title or Relationship*   *Address*

If the executor so chosen does not wish to serve, does not qualify, or
ceases at any time to act as executor, my spouse/son/daughter will have
the power to select a successor executor from the same list.

5. (Appointment conditioned on age) I appoint my spouse,
_____, and my son/daughter _____ as co-
executors [and co-trustees] on condition that my spouse survives me and
that my son/daughter has reached the age of 21 before my death. On
failure of either or both conditions, I appoint _____ as first
successor fiduciary and _____ as second successor
fiduciary.

6. (Property in different states) I name _____ as the
executor of my will as to my real property located in the state of
_____, and _____ as the executor of my will
as to all other property located elsewhere.

7. (Long form: person and institution as co-executors)

a. At all times during the administration of my estate, there shall be two
co-executors: an individual and an institution.

b. I nominate my spouse, _____, as individual executor; if
he/she is unable or unwilling to serve, I nominate _____ as
successor individual executor. The individual executor is to serve without
bond.

c. I nominate the _____ Bank and Trust Company of _____, or its corporate successor or assign, as institutional executor.

d. The institutional co-executor's duties include maintenance of estate records and accounts, and maintaining custody of all estate assets coming into either executor's possession.

e. The institutional executor is to receive the compensation it would receive as sole executor; the individual executor is to receive only such additional compensation as is allowed by the probate court.

f. Neither executor will be liable for the negligent or wrongful acts of the other executor.

g. My executors have authority and discretion to:

- sell, lease, or mortgage any part or all of my estate, on the terms they agree on
- retain any property or securities in the estate, in the form in which they entered the estate
- continue to manage any business property or investment property I owned at the time of my death.

No court order shall be required for any of these actions.

h. The profits and losses on estate transactions shall inure to the benefit or detriment of my estate, and not to my executors.

8. (Multiple fiduciaries) In case of disagreement between/among the executors or between/among the trustees, decisions shall be made by majority vote/_____ among the executors, _____ among the trustees, will have the casting vote/the decision of _____ will be final as to the following matters; the decision of _____ will be final as to all other matters.

NOTE: If multiple fiduciaires are appropriate, it's better to appoint an odd number of fiduciaries to minimize 1-1 or 2-2 splits.

9. (Exculpation for co-fiduciary acts) No fiduciary will be liable at any time for any action or failure or refusal to act undertaken in good faith and with the exercise of ordinary diligence. When there are multiple fiduciaries, no fiduciary will ever be liable for the negligence or wrongdoing of any other fiduciary, unless he/she/it participated in the act or permitted it to happen through failure to exercise ordinary diligence. No fiduciary will be liable for the negligence or wrongful acts of any agent who was appointed by a fiduciary exercising ordinary diligence.

EXECUTORS: COMPENSATION

NOTE: If the testator intends the statutory schedule of commissions to apply, no compensation clause is required.

1. (Bequest in lieu of commissions) To _____, I bequeath the amount of $_____ in return for his/her services as executor, and in lieu of any statutory commissions. [This bequest is conditional on his/her qualifying as executor and completing the duties of an executor.]

2. (Bequest in addition to commissions) In addition to the statutory commissions, I bequeath each of my executors the sum of $_____, payable when they qualify as executors/upon completion of their duties as executors.

NOTE: An amount payable when the executor qualifies is treated as a gift to the executor; an amount payable on completion of duties as an executor is treated as compensation—that is, as taxable income.

3. (Commission/no bond) If the probate court grants an order for the advance payment of executors' commissions, my wish is that the order be granted without requiring the executor to post bond.

4. (Employee compensation) Any fiduciary who is an employee, officer, or director of any business in which I have an ownership interest is entitled to receive and retain any compensation due him/her as an employee, officer, or director, in addition to his/her compensation as a fiduciary.

5. (Professional fees) Any fiduciary who is an attorney, broker, banker, financial planner, or consultant, and who renders such professional services to the estate/trust in addition to his/her duties as fiduciary, or whose professional partnership or corporate employer renders such services, shall be entitled to receive normal professional fees in addition to the statutory commissions or other compensation provided for his/her service as a fiduciary.

EXECUTORS: POWERS

1. (Administration expenses) My executor(s) shall have the power to pay all reasonable and proper expenses of administering my estate, including but not limited to attorneys' fees and the cost of bonding.

2. (Borrowing)...to borrow money, at rates not higher than market rates, for the limited purpose of carrying out the administration of my estate, and provided that proper security is given for the loan.

3. (Business belonging to testator)/(wind up business) I give my executor the power to wind up the business affairs of _____ [Inc.], the proprietorship/partnership/corporation in which I have a ____% interest. I direct the executor to do so on the most favorable terms possible, but in any case within six months of my death.

OR

My executor will have the discretion either to wind up the business affairs of _____, the closely held business of which I am President, or to continue such business in my place and stead, to the extent permitted by law.

NOTE: This clause would only be used if the executor is to inherit much of the estate, or if the executor can be trusted to manage the business with the testator's beneficiaries in mind. The phrase "to the extent permitted by law" deals with the situation in which, for example, the testator is licensed to practice a profession, but the executor is not; or if a crucial license is not transferable.

4. (Business belonging to testator/estate assets) My executor shall/may, in his or her discretion/shall not use other assets of my estate not invested in such business, for purposes of continuing, operating, and managing the business (e.g., using other estate assets as collateral or security for business indebtedness).

CROSS-REFERENCE: See Closely Held Business

5. (Distributions) I direct my executor to make all distributions in cash, not in kind

OR

My executor shall have full discretion (bearing in mind, however, the wishes of my legatees to the extent he/she thinks practicable) to make distributions in kind, in cash at market value, or partly in cash and partly in kind. On the same condition, he/she may allocate items of property among the recipients of a group of items, and need not consider the basis of such items in making the allocation.

6. (Exchanges)...to exchange property on whatever terms he/she believes to be appropriate.

NOTE: This clause may be desirable, because the statutory executor's power is probably a power to sell assets, not to exchange them.

7. (Investments)...to invest and reinvest such property in investment media including but not limited to common stocks, preferred stocks, mortgages and mortgage-backed securities, certificates of deposit, income-producing real estate, corporate and government bonds, and mutual fund shares. The executor is expressly permitted to invest in media outside the "legal list," provided that he/she abides by the standards of prudence and preservation of capital required of a fiduciary.

OR

The executor may not invest more than ____% of the total assets of the estate in the securities of any one issuer; provided, however, that the executor may invest any amount in government or government-backed securities, and may invest up to ____% in a single mutual fund.

Furthermore, if the securities of a given issuer represent more than ____% of the value of the estate because they have increased in value relative to other estate assets in the time since their purchase, divestiture will not be required.

OR

My executor may retain any investment which is an estate asset at the time of my death, and which is not on the "legal list." However, this power to retain does not give my executor the right to make any new investments outside the "legal list."

8. (Insurance)...to purchase and/or maintain insurance (e.g., fire, casualty, title, liability) in amounts and on terms adequate to protect the property of the trust while it is under administration, and to indemnify the executor him/her/itself.

9. (Pourovers)...to accept additions to my estate from sources other than myself and insurance payable to my estate.

10. (Q-Tip) I give to my executor the absolute discretion to treat all or a specific part of any eligible property as "Q-Tip" property.

OR

I direct my executor to treat the following property/the specified portion of the following property as "Q-Tip" property:

11. (Real estate) If any part of my estate consists of real property, my executors will have the right to sell, mortgage, lease, transfer, or convey any such property, to pay real estate, transfer, and other taxes on the property; to maintain the property in habitable and saleable condition; to apply for zoning variances on the property; to act as mortgagee of the property, as they see fit.

OR

...to lease, sublease, or mortgage any real or personal property in the estate for a duration and at terms of his/her discretion, without regard to statutory restrictions, and with no necessity for court approval.

12. (Successors) Any power or discretion in excess of the statutory powers granted to a fiduciary by this instrument will be equally applicable to successor fiduciaries.

13. (Tax returns)...to join with my surviving spouse (or the executor of his/her estate) in filing a joint tax return for any open years up to and including the year of my death; and to consent to any gift made by my spouse in the year of my death being treated as a split gift.

FUNERAL AND BURIAL INSTRUCTIONS

1. (Funeral expenses) I direct that my executor pay the costs of my last illness and funeral [with a limit, however, of $_____ for funeral expenses] as an expense of administration.

NOTE: Some state laws obligate the surviving spouse to pay last-illness and funeral expenses, unless exonerated.

2. (Prepaid funeral expenses) My executor is charged with paying all my just debts out of the assets of my estate. This direction applies to the expenses of my last illness and of my funeral, but I direct the attention of my executor to the existence of a prepaid funeral arrangement with the _____ funeral home, whose address is _____, evidenced by contract #_____, dated _____, 19_____.

3. (Funeral instructions) A set of written instructions for my funeral is on file at the _____ Mortuary located at _____. These instructions are hereby incorporated into this will by reference. I direct that these instructions be followed to the extent possible.

4. (Anatomical gift) I, _____, am over 18 and wish that, after my death, my body/kidneys/corneas/any organ or body part needed be transferred to the _____ Medical School/_____ Dental School/_____ organ bank for the purpose of transplantation/therapy/research/medical or dental education.

NOTE: Of course, the family must be aware of the intention to make an anatomical gift—otherwise, the funeral could take place before the intention to make an anatomical gift even becomes known.

5. (Cremation) I direct that my body be cremated, and my ashes placed in niche _____ in the _____ Mausoleum, in a suitable urn to be purchased by my executor.

6. (Burial plot) If I do not own a cemetery plot at the time of death, I direct my executor to buy a suitable plot in _____ Cemetery; if no such plot is available, in a cemetary chosen by the executor. The plot shall be large enough for my own interment/for the interment of myself and _____ members of my immediate family. I further direct my executor to sign a perpetual care agreement covering the plot, and to make the payment or payments necessary to fund such perpetual care. [However, in no event shall the total cost of the burial plot and perpetual care exceed $_____.]

7. (Monument/gravestone) My executor is directed to buy a gravestone or monument, of a type and material suitable for the _____ section of _____ cemetery, and to pay for the stone/ monument at its placement out of the assets of my estate. The cost is not to be less than $_____, or more than $_____. The stone/ monument is to be inscribed as follows:

The stone/monument is to be placed within _____ days of my death/one year after my burial.

GUARDIANSHIP

1. (Person and property) If I am survived by my spouse, and if he/she dies while any of our children is still a minor and without appointing a guardian, I designate my brother and sister-in-law, _____, as guardians of the person and property of any minor children. If my brother and his wife do not survive my spouse, or if they are not married and continuing to live together at the time of my spouse's death, I designate my spouse's brother and sister-in-law, _____, as guardians of the person and property of any minor children.

2. (Separate guardians) In the event that I am not survived by my spouse, or if my spouse dies while any of our children are still minors, and has not appointed a guardian for them, I designate my sister, _____, as guardian of the person of any minor children. I designate my attorney, _____ Esq., of the firm of _____, as guardian of the property of any minor children.

IN TERROREM

1. (As if predeceased) If any person named as a beneficiary under this will institutes a will contest, acts as a party to a will contest initiated by someone else, or aids and abets anyone instituting a will contest, I direct that any bequest, devise, or share of my residuary estate that would otherwise go to that person shall lapse, as if he or she had predeceased me.

2. (Divided among non-contestants) The share of my estate given by this will to any beneficiary who contests the will in whole or in part shall be revoked, and shall be divided among the beneficiaries who do *not* contest the will, in proportions corresponding to their proportional share of the original probate estate.

OR

Whoever shall contest this will, participate in a will contest, or attempt to invalidate any provision of this will, shall forfeit all gifts, bequests, and interests under this will. The amount so forfeited shall be divided among the will beneficiaries who did not contest the will, in proportion to their share of the probate estate as a whole.

If all the beneficiaries contest the will or participate in a will contest, I direct that my entire estate be paid to the _____ Dog and Cat Hospital or its successors.

INTRODUCTIONS

1. (General) This is the will of _____, a U.S. citizen who lives at _____. I have been married to _____ since _____, 19____. ____ children have been born to this relationship: _____, born _____, 19____ [etc.] We adopted a child, _____, born _____, 19____, on _____, 19____; and _____, born _____, 19____, a child of my/my spouse's earlier marriage also lives with us. All references to my "children" include all these children equally.

2. (Statement of heirship) I have no living or predeceased children; neither of my parents is alive; I have no [surviving] siblings. If I were to die on the date of this will, the following people would be my sole heirs at law, to the best of my knowledge:

Name   *Relationship*   *Address [if known]*

LAPSE

1. (To other beneficiaries) If the gifts to any of the beneficiaries mentioned in this Section, of the will would otherwise lapse, I direct that the gift be divided among the other beneficiaries of this Section, in proportion to their interest in the property disposed of by this Section/in proportion to their interest in the residue of my estate.

2. (Under dead beneficiary's will) If _____ does not survive me, but dies leaving a valid will, I direct that the bequest to him/her be distributed to the people, and in the proportions, specified by the residuary clause of his/her will.

3 (To dead beneficiary's spouse; child of testator) To my son/daughter _____, I leave $_____/the following articles: _____ if he/she survives me; if he/she does not survive me, to his or her spouse.

OR

If my son/daughter dies before I do, and is survived by a spouse, but no children, I direct that my son/daughter's share be paid to his/her spouse. If my son/daughter dies before I do and is survived by a spouse and child or children, I direct that my son/daughter's share be divided into equal shares, one for the spouse and one for each child.

MARRIAGE DOES NOT REVOKE

1. Although I am not now married, I plan to marry _____ on or about _____, 19____. This will is executed in contemplation of marriage, and I do not intend that this will be revoked by my marriage.

RELEASE OF DEBTS

1. (Beneficiary) I hereby release all claims and extinguish all debts which I may have against, or which may be owed to me by, any person who is a beneficiary under my will.

2. (Specific debt) I hereby release _____ from all claims I or my successors may have against him/her under a note/mortgage dated _____, 19____, bearing an original face amount of $_____, and I hereby forgive any debt under such instrument remaining at the time of my death, including/except for payments in default and overdue interest.

CROSS-REFERENCE: See "just debts" under DEFINITIONS.

3. (Long form) I cancel and release all debts owed to me by _____ on the date of my death. If he/she predeceases me, this release will benefit his/her estate.

I direct my executor to mark all documents evidencing the obligation "cancelled" and return them to the debtor or his/her personal representative, as soon after my death as practicable. I also direct my executor to carry out any other act required to effectuate or prove the release and discharge, and return any security to the debtor or his/her estate.

SEVERABILITY

1. I direct that any portion of this will that is construed or held to be invalid be severed from the rest of the will, and that the remaining, valid portions of the will be given full effect according to their terms.

SURVIVORSHIP AND COMMON DISASTER

1. (Spouse/revoked if dies within 6 months) As a condition of all bequests made by my spouse, I direct that, if he/she survives me by less than six months, that any portion of the bequest which he/she did not sell or transfer during the period between our deaths be returned to be estate and be distributed as if my spouse had predeceased me. However, all income earned on the property after my death and before hers/his shall be treated as her/his property and not subject to return to my estate.

2. (Spouse/reduced if dies within 6 months) I devise and bequeath the entire residue of my estate, including lapsed dispositions and property over which I have a power of appointment, to my spouse, _____, if he/she survives me.

    However, if he/she survives me but dies within six months of my death, I direct that the gift of the residue of my estate be divested, and that, instead, he/she receive $_____, payable entirely and only in property and proceeds qualifying for the federal estate tax marital deduction.

    If my spouse and I die under circumstances rendering it impossible to determine who died first, I direct that it be presumed that I died first, and my will is to be construed as if my spouse survived me.

3. (Common disaster/any beneficiary) If any beneficiary of my will dies as a result of the common disaster causing my death/within _____ days of my death/within _____ months of my death, I direct that the property bequeathed or devised to him/her be paid to his/her surviving spouse/be paid to his/her children per capita/be paid to his/her children per stripes/ become part of my residuary estate.

UGMA

1. (UGMA Gift) I, _____, hereby deliver the following
( ) tangible personal property:
( ) real estate:
( ) securities:
to _____, who is custodian under the Uniform Gift to
Minors Act for _____, a minor born _____, 19___.

Date: Signature:

I, _____, hereby acknowledge receipt of the
_____ described above as UGMA custodian for
_____.

Date   Signature:

REVOCABLE INTER VIVOS TRUST

a. The grantor is _____, whose residence is
_____; the trustee is _____, whose residence/
home office is _____.

b. This document expresses the terms on which _____ will
act as trustee of a revocable *inter vivos* trust hereby created by the
grantor.

c. The grantor assigns, transfers, and conveys the "trust property" to the
trustee, who acknowledges its receipt and agrees to hold and manage the
trust property pursuant to the terms of this trust agreement.

d. The grantor, or any other person, may add to the trust property by
transferring additional property to the trustee, by making insurance
proceeds payable to the trustee, and/or by pourover by will.

e. The "trust property" is as follows: _____/is set out in
Exhibit A, which is hereby incorporated by reference.

f. This trust agreement may be amended or revoked by the grantor at any
time, by stating the terms of the amendment or revocation in writing
delivered to the trustee. However, all amendments or revocations affecting
real property must be acknowledged in the same manner as a conveyance
eligible to be recorded. Furthermore, no amendment may increase the
duties and/or liabilities of the trustee without the trustee's prior written
consent.

g. The trustee shall hold, manage, invest, and reinvest the trust property,
and distribute the net income to the following persons as income
beneficiaries: _____ as follows: _____.

h. The term of the trust shall be ____ years/until _____
reaches the age of ____ or dies/for 21 years after the death of the
grantor's youngest grandchild living when this trust agreement is
executed. After the term of the trust, the trust will terminate and the
trustee shall pay the remaining trust property and any accumulated
income to _____, the remainderman.

i. Net income is defined as gross income of the trust less the trustee's
compensation, necessary expenses of trust management and investment,
and income taxes imposed on the trust.

j. After the grantor's death, the trustee has full and sole discretion to
invade the principal of the trust for the education, medical treatment, or
support of the income beneficiary(ies)/the following of the income
beneficiaries: _____. [However, I direct the trustee to avoid
invading trust principal for any sum otherwise payable or reimbursable by
Medicare or Medicaid.]

k. Any mandatory or discretionary distribution to a minor may be made
by:

  • making the distribution to the minor's parent or guardian

- making an expenditure to a third party [e.g., school or college, health care provider] for the benefit of the minor
- accumulating income applicable to the minor's use in the trust, payable to the minor when he/she reaches majority.

l. The trustee shall receive the statutory compensation as provided by §_____ of the laws of the state of _____.

m. The trustee shall have all the powers provided by statute, and the following additional powers:

- To hire attorneys, accountants, financial planners, and other professionals; to pay them reasonable compensation
- To receive reimbursement from trust principal or income (at his/her/its discretion, for personal/corporate funds expended for the reasonable expenses of trust investment and administration
- To deal with third parties with no requirement that the third party investigate the trustee's authority to enter into a transaction or apply the proceeds of a transaction.

n. During the grantor's life, he/she has full power to remove the trustee and make a written nomination of the successor trustee. After the grantor's death, _____ will have this power.

The trustee, in turn, may resign at any time by written notice to the grantor or to _____ after the grantor's death.

After the trustee's removal or resignation, and before he/she/it has rendered accounts, had the accounts settled, and been discharged, the trustee will continue to have all statutory powers and all powers granted by this trust agreement. All powers and duties will vest in the successor trustee as soon as the original trustee is discharged, and as soon as he/she/it signs a written acceptance of the office of trustee.

o. This trust indenture benefits and binds the grantor and his/her estate, executor, successors, and assigns, and the trustee and his, her, or its successors and assigns.

Q-TIP TRUST

a. If my spouse survives me (by _____ days) the trustee shall divide the residue of my estate/the trust property described above/the assets of my *inter vivos* trust poured over to my probate estate into two trusts. One trust shall be a "marital trust"; the other shall be a "residuary trust."

b. The marital trust shall consist entirely of assets qualifying for the federal estate tax marital deduction, in an amount equal to the excess of the taxable estate over the available unified credit. The trustee is directed to apportion appreciated and depreciated property equitably (though not necessarily equally) between the two trusts.

c. The residuary trust shall consist of all assets in the trust estate and not forming part of the marital trust.

d. The trustee shall pay the net income of the marital trust to my spouse at least once a year, or shall apply it for his/her benefit.

e. The trustee shall pay/pay and accumulate the net income of the residuary trust as follows: _____ _____

f. When my spouse dies, the trustee shall distribute the principal and accumulated income of both trusts as follows: _____

CROSS-REFERENCE: See DISTRIBUTIONS, TRUST A-TRUST B ARRANGEMENT.

CLIFFORD TRUST

a. _____ ("grantor") hereby transfers the following property ("trust corpus") to _____ (the "trustee"). The grantor's intention is to create an irrevocable Clifford trust for the benefit of _____ ("beneficiary").

b. The trust will continue either for ten years and one day from the date of execution, or until the death of the beneficiary, whichever event occurs first.

c. During the trust term, the trustee will pay all net trust income to the beneficiary, or apply it for the beneficiary's benefit. Payments to a minor beneficiary, or for a beneficiary whom the trustee, in his/her/its absolute discretion believes to be incompetent (whether or not a judicial determination of incompetence has been made) may be made, in the trustee's discretion:

- directly to the beneficiary
- to the beneficiary's guardian, conservator, or other fiduciary
- to the person or organization furnishing a home for the beneficiary
- directly to providers of care, support, maintenance, and/or education to the beneficiary. In this context, "education" includes post-secondary, vocational, and professional education, and also includes the beneficiary's reasonable living expenses while he/she is a student.

A receipt furnished by the direct payee will discharge the trustee completely, and the trustee has no obligation to administer such funds once they have been paid.

d. On _____, 19____ (or on the earlier death of the beneficiary) the trust will terminate, and the trustee will pay all undistributed income to the beneficiary (or to the beneficiary's estate, if he/she is dead) and the trust corpus to the grantor (or the grantor's executor or administrator if he/she is dead).

NOTE: The Tax Code of 1986 removes the income-splitting advantages formerly obtainable from Clifford Trusts.

TWO-TRUST APPROACH (MARITAL AND NON-MARITAL TRUSTS)

a. It is my intention to prevent the imposition of federal estate tax on my estate and that of my spouse, if he/she survives me, to the greatest extent permitted by law. To this end, I direct my executor-trustee to divide my entire estate [except for the bequests detailed above] into two trusts.

b. Trust A, the residuary trust, is to consist of assets equivalent in value to the unified credit available to my estate. I direct that the trustee pay the net income of Trust A, at least once a year, in equal shares to those of my children who survive me.

c. Trust B, the marital trust, is to consist of the rest and residue of my estate. I direct that the trustee distribute the net income of Trust B to my spouse at least once a year.

d. Trust B is to terminate on my spouse's death, at which time the trustee will distribute the remaining trust principal and accrued income to whomever my spouse appoints by will or by deed. If he/she does not so appoint, to my children then surviving in equal shares.

e. Trust A is to terminate when any of my children who survived me dies. I direct my trustee to distribute the remaining trust principal and accrued income to my children then surviving, in equal shares.

f. I direct the trustee to fund Trust B only with assets qualifying for the federal estate tax marital deduction.

OR

a. I direct the trustee to pay the net income of both trusts to my spouse at least once a year, or apply the net income of both trusts for his/her support, comfort, and medical care.

b. When, in the discretion of my trustees, my spouse requires funds in addition to his/her own assets, net trust income, and Social Security in order to maintain a comfortable style of life, the trustee may invade trust principal. However, I direct that the marital trust be invaded first, and that the residuary trust not be invaded as long as there are any assets in the marital trust.

CROSS-REFERENCE: See INVASION.

NOTE: It's more conventional to refer to the marital trust as Trust A, the residuary trust as Trust B. However, this nomenclature was established before the unlimited marital deduction, when the funding of the marital trust had to be defined in pecuniary or fractional terms.

CHARITABLE REMAINDER UNITRUST

a. My intention is to create a charitable remainder unitrust qualifying for the federal estate tax charitable deduction. I intend to benefit _____ as beneficiary and _____ as charitable remainderman. All provisions of my will, and all actions of my trustee, are to be construed and taken with this objective in mind.

b. I give, devise, and bequeath _____ to my trustee, in trust, to be held, invested, reinvested, and managed in order to pay the "unitrust amount" to my beneficiary. Payment is to be made at least annually, starting at the date of my death.

c. Any excess of trust income over the unitrust amount is to be added to principal.

However, I direct the trustee to pay the excess income to the beneficiary until the aggregate income paid in past years equals ____% of the trust corpus' fair market value for each year, times the number of years the trust has been in existence.

d. The unitrust amount for each year equals ____% of the fair market value of the trust corpus on the first day of that year/the smaller of the trust income or ____% of the fair market value of the trust corpus on the first day of that year.

e. Neither trustee's commissions nor estate taxes may be charged against the unitrust amount. *NOTE: See Rev. Rul. 74-19, 1974-1 CB 155 and Rev. Rul. 82-128, 1982-2 CB 71.*

NOTE: Under Reg. §1.664-3(b), a charitable remainder unitrust can accept pourovers, but a charitable remainder annuity trust cannot. (Reg. §1-664.2(b).

CHARITABLE REMAINDER ANNUITY TRUST

a. It is my intention to create a trust qualifying for the federal estate tax charitable remainder deduction. Therefore, I direct that all provisions of this will be construed so as to carry out this intention, and that the trustee refrain from using his/her/its discretion or powers as trustee in any way that would render this deduction unavailable.

b. With this intention in mind, I give, devise, and bequeath _____ to my trustee(s) in trust, for the purposes described below in Section ____ of this will. Other than excess income, there will be no additional funding of this trust.

c. I direct the trustee to hold, manage, invest, reinvest, and collect the income from the trust property, and pay the annuity amount to my spouse/son/daughter/friend _____ (the "beneficiary") at least once a year, starting on the date of my death, and ending with the beneficiary's death. NOTE: See Rev. Rul. 80-123, 1980-1 CB 205. The trustee will have the power to sell assets and to realize capital gains.

d. The "annuity amount" is ____% of the initial net fair market value of the trust assets as finally determined for federal estate tax purposes.

NOTE: Code §664 requires that the percentage be five percent or over.

e. If the trust's income in any taxable year exceeds the annuity amount, the trustee is to add the excess to the trust principal.

f. If, at any time, there has been an underpayment or overpayment as defined by Reg. §1.664-1(a)(5) or its successor provision, I direct the trustee to pay any underpayment to, or demand any overpayment from, the beneficiary within a reasonable time after the event.

g. In the year of the beneficiary's death, the trustee is to prorate the annuity amount for the short taxable year. Proration is to be done on a daily basis as provided by Reg. §1.664-2 or its successor provision.

h. The trustee is further directed to make any distributions required for the trust to avoid taxation under Code §4942; to avoid investments taxable under Code §4944; to dispose of any property which would otherwise be treated as excess business holdings under Code §4943(c); and to refrain from all acts of self-dealing penalized by Code §4941(d), except as required to pay the annuity amount to the beneficiary. All references to Code provisions are to the provisions as amended from time to time.

i. On the death of the beneficiary, I direct the trustee to terminate the trust and distribute all trust corpus and accumulated income, less any amount due the beneficiary but not yet paid, to _____, the charitable beneficiary, to be used for its general charitable purposes. However, if the charitable beneficiary is not then a "charity" as defined by Code §2055(a) as amended, I direct the trustee to select the "charity" nearest in purpose, achievements, and organizational style, to _____, and distribute the trust principal and accrued income to it.

TRUST FOR MINOR (PRESENT INTEREST)

a. The trustee shall pay or distribute principal and income [after taxes and all fees and expenses of administration] to or for the benefit of
_____, a minor ("the beneficiary").

b. Until the beneficiary reaches age 21 [unless he/she dies sooner], the trustee shall pay the trust's net income to or for the benefit of the beneficiary annually/quarterly/monthly.

c. The trustee also has absolute discretion to invade principal at any time and in any amount, and distribute such principal to or for the benefit of the beneficiary.

d. The trustee has absolute discretion to make any payment or expenditure in any one of four ways:

- To the beneficiary him/herself
- To the beneficiary's guardian or any fiduciary of the beneficiary's person or estate
- To a person or organization providing a home for the beneficiary
- To any one providing goods or services to the beneficiary.

A receipt given by any payee will discharge the trustee completely, and the trustee has no obligation to administer such funds once they are paid.

e. The trust will terminate on the earlier of the beneficiary's death or his/her 21st birthday. If it terminates by death, all principal and accumulated income will be paid to the beneficiary's estate; if it terminates by the beneficiary's majority, all principal and accumulated income will be paid to the beneficiary.

NOTE: Under Code §§677(b), and (c), a parent-trustee will not be taxable on trust income power to use trust income for support obligations, but will be taxed if the income is in fact so applied.

For accumulation power add to (b):
The trustee has sole and entire discretion to distribute trust principal and income, or accumulate trust income, during the entire term of the trust.

For accumulation trust, substitute:

a. I give the sum of $_____ to my trustee in trust, for the benefit of my son/daughter, _____.

b. From the time of my death until he/she reaches the age of 18/21, I direct the trustee to manage, invest, and reinvest this sum, and to make quarterly payments of $_____ each to my son's/daughter's guardian to be used for his/her support and education.

c. Any income in excess of the quarterly payments is to be accumulated, and the trust corpus and accumulated income are to be paid to my son/daughter as soon as possible after his/her 18th/21st birthday.

d. If he/she dies before reaching the age of 21/18, the trust corpus and accumulated income are to be paid to my younger son/older daughter, _____, as soon as possible after my death.

REVOCABLE UNFUNDED INSURANCE TRUST

a. Grantor, _____, hereby transfers the following insurance policies on his/her life to _____, the trustee. The trustee acknowledges receipt of the policies and agrees to hold them and any policies or other property later transferred by the grantor in a revocable trust pursuant to the terms of this agreement.

b. As long as he/she is alive, the grantor may deal with the policies as if this trust had never been created, and may:

- surrender any policy and receive its cash value
- borrow against the policy
- convert it into any other form of policy.

c. The grantor is responsible for paying the premiums on the policies, and will have and maintain the policies payable to the trustee in his/her/its capacity as trustee.

d. The trustee will hold the policies for safekeeping during the grantor's life, but will not be responsible for paying the premiums or maintaining the policies in force.

e. When the grantor dies, the trustee will use his/her/its best efforts to collect the policy proceeds (including any available double indemnity benefits) but may, in his/her/its discretion, permit any amount of the proceeds to remain with the insurer pursuant to a settlement option. The trustee will not be liable for losses attributable to the selection of a settlement option.

f. The trustee will apply all proceeds received in lump sums, and all assets "poured over" from the grantor's will, as follows:

- If the grantor's estate is insufficient to pay the estate's debts, administration expenses, and taxes, the trustee will advance the necessary funds to the executor.
- During the trust terms (of _____ years/until the following event occurs: _____) the trustee will hold, invest, reinvest, and manage the insurance proceeds and pourover property, and will pay or apply the income as follows:_____ _____

On termination of the trust, the trustee will pay and distribute the remaining trust principal and accumulated income as follows:_____

g. The grantor may revoke this trust at any time, without consent or notice to any beneficiary, by filing a written revocation with the trustee, and releasing and indemnifying the trustee with respect to all obligations and claims under this trust.

h. The grantor may amend this trust (including changing beneficiaries or limiting their rights) on written consent of the trustee.

NOTE: The insurance company may require filing of the trust agreement before making policy payments in accordance with the trust terms.

IRREVOCABLE LIFE INSURANCE TRUST

a. The grantor hereby transfers to the trustee the following insurance policies on the grantor's life: _____ and the following other property: _____ to fund this irrevocable trust for the benefit of _____.

b. During the grantor's lifetime, the trustee will hold the insurance policies and invest the other trust assets. The trustee will apply the trust's net income to the payment of the premiums of the policies in the trust, and will accumulate any additional net income.

c. The trustee will inform the grantor if, at any time, net income is insufficient to pay the premiums. If, given this notice, the grantor does not provide the necessary funds, the trustee, may in his sole and complete discretion,

- sell part of the non-insurance trust assets by public or private sale
- borrow, using non-insurance trust assets as collateral
- take out policy loans on any insurance policy in the trust
- surrender any policy in the trust for its cash surrender value
- convert any policy to a paid-up policy in whatever amount can be obtained in return for accrued premium payments.

The trustee is not obligated to pay such premiums, and is not liable if they are not paid.

d. When the grantor dies, the trustee will undertake any acts necessary to collect the proceeds of the insurance policies in the trust (including any available double indemnity payments). The proceeds, once collected, will become part of the trust principal.

e. When the grantor dies, the trustee will distribute the trust principal and accrued income as follows: _____ _____

CROSS-REFERENCE: See DISTRIBUTION.

f. In addition to all statutory powers, the trustee shall have the power (but not the obligation) to apply the dividends on insurance policies in the trust to reduce future premiums. If the trustee chooses not to do this, the dividends will become part of the trust income.

TRUST TO PROVIDE COLLEGE SCHOLARSHIPS

a. I give the sum of $_____ to _____ College, located in _____, or to its successor institution.

b. This sum and its accumulated income are to be held by the college in trust, invested, and reinvested.

c. The net trust income is to be used at least every other year to furnish a scholarship for a student selected by the Dean of Students of _____ College.

d. Such selection is to be made without discrimination by race, religion, sex, or national origin, and shall be made to benefit a student talented in the performing arts/demonstrating athletic ability and sportsmanship/pursuing premedical studies/returning to college after raising a family/who would otherwise be unable to attend _____ College for financial reasons.

e. This scholarship is to be known as the _____ Scholarship.

f. If at any time _____ College ceases to function as a four-year college and has no successor, or if at any time the trust income ceases to be used to provide a scholarship, I direct that the trust principal and any accumulated income be paid to my eldest grandchild then living/the American Red Cross/my issue then surviving per stirpes.

NOTE: In some states (New York, for example) a trust of this type is subject to registration and annual reporting requirements.

ACCUMULATION AND DISTRIBUTION

1. (Accumulation) I direct that the trustee accumulate the net income generated by the trust corpus for the benefit of _____ (the "income beneficiary") for the following period: _____.

    On expiration of the trust term, the trust will end, and the trustee will pay the trust corpus to the beneficiary if he/she is still alive. This payment will be absolute and not in further trust.

    If the income beneficiary dies during the trust term, I direct the trustee to pay the trust corpus and accumulated income to the income beneficiary's estate/to _____/to my issue then surviving, per stirpes/to the income beneficiary's surviving children, in equal shares. This payment will be absolute, and not in further trust.

2. (Split distribution) When _____ reaches the age of 21/25/30, he/she is to receive one half of the trust principal. When he/she reaches the age of 26/30/35, he/she is to receive the remaining trust principal plus any accumulated income.

    If he/she dies before reaching 26/30/35, the trustee is to pay the remaining principal plus accumulated income, as appointed by the beneficiary by will. If he/she died intestate or without exercising the power, the principal and accumulated income are to be paid to

_____.

3. (Spray power) a. The "class of beneficiaries" includes my spouse, _____, and our children [including children alive at the making of this will, afterborn and posthumous children, and including/but excluding adopted children].

b. In his/her/its/their discretion, the trustee(s) may distribute trust income and principal to any member(s) of the class of beneficiaries, or may apply it for their support, maintenance, education, and/or health care OR may distribute trust income and principal whenever a beneficiary's net income falls below $_____, or whenever a beneficiary or a beneficiary's parent or guardian, on the beneficiary's behalf, incurs expenses of education and/or medical care in excess of $_____ in any one year.

c. Distributions may be made in cash or in kind. The trustee(s) is/are not required to equalize distributions among or for the benefit of the various beneficiaries, and is/are not required to take the other financial resources or sources of income into account. Distributions to the income beneficiaries need not be taken into account if and when they become entitled to distribution of principal. The trustee's discretion shall be final and absolute.

d. Any income that is not so paid or applied shall be added to the trust principal/invested and reinvested in safe, short-term fixed-income investments. [In exercising this spray power, I request that the trustee consult the wishes of the following members of my family who are not trust beneficiaries: _____. However, this request is precatory, not mandatory.]

e. The trustee is independent of me, the grantor, and is not related to or subordinate to me. No one can add to the list of beneficiaries.

NOTE: See Code §674(c).

DURATION

1. (Term of years) The trustee shall pay the income of the trust to
_____ for a period of _____ years from my death, or until the beneficiary's death, whichever is earlier. When the trust ends, the trustee shall pay over the principal and any accrued income to

_____.

2. (Measured by beneficiary's age) I direct the trustee to pay the trust's income to the beneficiary at least quarterly until his death, or until his twenty-fifth birthday. On the beneficiary's twenty-fifth birthday, I direct the trustee to distribute the trust corpus plus accumulated income to the beneficiary. On his death before reaching the age of 25, I direct the trustee to distribute the trust corpus plus accumulated income to

_____.

3. (Perpetuities saving clause) However, any trust created by this will/this instrument must terminate not later than twenty-one years after the death of the youngest beneficiary who was alive at the time of my death/the creation of this trust. On termination, the trust principal and accumulated income are to be distributed as follows:

INVASION

a. (Standard) I direct the trustee to apply his/her/its discretion generously, and to invade principal whenever necessary to provide a comfortable standard of living for _____, not merely to provide the necessities of life.

b. (Supplement Social Security) It is my intention that my spouse, _____, be able to rely on a monthly income of at least $_____. Therefore, if at any time the monthly trust income payable to my spouse, added to his/her monthly Social Security benefit payment is less than $_____, I direct my trustee to invade principal until the total income from the trust, Social Security benefit, and payment from principal equals $_____.

c. (Request if income fails to reach minimum) However, if the trust's net income falls below $_____ in any calendar year, and if the beneficiary makes a written request before April 1 of the next calendar year, the trustee is to invade principal and pay either the amount requested or the difference between $_____ and net income, whichever is smaller. The right to request is not cumulative: that is, if it is not exercised in a given year it lapses, and requests may not be made in later years to make up for the deficiency.

OR

If the trust's net income for any calendar year is less than $_____, I direct the trustee to invade the trust principal so that the total payments of net income plus principal made to the trust beneficiary in any calendar year equal $_____, until the trust principal is exhausted.

In the year of my death, and in the year of my spouse's death, this amount shall be prorated on a daily basis.

d. (Absolute right to demand) On written demand from my spouse/anyone in the class of beneficiaries, the trustee will pay over any part or the whole of the trust principal as demanded by the beneficiary.

NOTE: Under Code §678(a), trust capital gains are taxable to an income beneficiary who has unrestricted power to demand invasion, because this right is treated as an ownership interest. Under §2041(b), the right to demand invasion is equivalent to a power of appointment. Therefore, the trust principal will be included in the beneficiary's estate unless it is a "5-or-5" power or unless the demand is limited by an ascertainable standard relating to the beneficiary's health, education, support, or maintenance.

e. ("5-or-5") My spouse/anyone in the class of beneficiaries may serve the trustee with a written demand for invasion of the trust principal. The trustee is directed to comply promptly with any such demand falling into either of these categories:

- A demand which, when aggregated with all other demands he/she made during that calendar year, does not exceed the *greater* of $5,000 or 5% of the fair market value of the trust principal. The trust principal is to be valued as off January 1 of the calendar year of the demand(s).

- Sums the beneficiary deems necessary for his/her support, maintenance, health care, or education in order to maintain the standard of living he/she enjoyed while I was alive. (Such demands may be made and satisfied regardless of the beneficiary's own income and resources from other sources.)

f. (Crummey power) In each calendar year, the beneficiary may demand and receive from the trustee either $_____ or the total of *inter vivos* gifts made to the trust that year, whichever is smaller. The trustee is directed to inform the beneficiary of all *inter vivos* gifts within 10 days of the trustee's receipt of the gift. Payment shall be made from the property transferred to the trust by way of *inter vivos* gift, and may be in either cash or kind at the trustee's discretion.

Demand may be made by, and payment made to, the guardian or conservator of a beneficiary who lacks legal capacity. If the trustee receives a demand from a beneficiary lacking legal capacity, and who has neither conservator nor guardian, the trustee will use his/her/its best efforts to have a conservator or guardian appointed.

All of the trustee's actions must benefit the beneficiary rather than the grantor. The grantor may not borrow any trust assets at any time without paying market rates of interest and furnishing adequate security, and may not deal with or dispose of trust assets except for adequate and full consideration and on terms that would prevail in an arms-length transaction. Specifically, the trustee is forbidden to use trust income to buy a life insurance policy on the grantor's life.

g. (Invasion for accident or illness) The trustee may, in his/her/its discretion, invade the trust principal if my spouse's illness, or an accident involving him/her creates a need for additional funds for health care and/ or to replace lost income. (The trustee need not consider my spouse's other income and resources before invading the principal/with the provision, however, that principal not be invaded to pay any amount that would otherwise be payable or reimbursable by Medicare or Medicaid.)

h. (No invasion by trustee-beneficiary) No original or successor trustee who is also a beneficiary shall have any right or power to participate in any decision by the trustees as to when, or for whose benefit, the trust principal is to be invaded.

i. (Limitations on invasion) However, invasion of principal in any calendar year is not to exceed _____% of the fair market value of the trust principal, as measured on January 1 of the year of the withdrawal/to exceed $_____ in any calendar year.

OR

However, once the aggregate invasions of principal exceed $_____/_____% of the fair market value of the trust principal, as measured as of the date of my death, no further invasions of principal will be permitted.

IRREVOCABLE TRUST (INTRODUCTION)

1. _____, the grantor, hereby transfers the following property: _____ to _____, the trustee, who acknowledges its receipt. This property (the "trust principal") will be held and managed by the trustee, and will be applied as mandated by the grantor of this trust instrument.

2. This trust is irrevocable, and its terms are not subject to amendment or alteration by any person.

SPENDTHRIFT CLAUSE

1. (Title does not vest) During the trust term, title to the trust principal and unpaid trust income does not vest in the beneficiary. The beneficiary has no power or authority to alienate, anticipate, transfer, or convey such principal or unpaid income. Neither shall any creditor of the beneficiary have the right to involuntarily alienate, attach, execute, or levy upon trust principal or unpaid income.

2. (Limits on beneficiary rights) No trust beneficiary shall have the right or power to assign, anticipate, or alienate any income payable under any testamentary trust created by this will. Nor shall trust income be subject to claims made by the creditor of any beneficiary.

SPOUSE'S ELECTIVE SHARE IN TRUST

a. If my spouse, _____, survives me, I leave to my trustees, in trust, an amount equal to my spouse's elective share in my estate, minus any other property passing to my spouse under this will or otherwise. I direct that my trustees hold, manage, invest, and reinvest this property and pay its net income to my spouse at least quarterly, for his/ her lifetime. The trustees shall have the power to invade the principal of the trust, within their discretion, for my spouse's support, benefit, and comfort. However, my spouse has no power to demand such invasion of principal.

b. Furthermore, I direct my trustees to *avoid* invading principal to pay medical expenses of my spouse that would be covered by Medicaid if there were no invasion of principal.

c. On the death of my spouse, the trustees shall distribute the principal and accumulated income of the trust to such of our children as survive my spouse, in equal shares.

TERMINATION OF TRUST BY TRUSTEE

a. I, _____ am the trustee of a trust known as the _____ trust, created by _____ on _____, 19____ to benefit _____ as income beneficiary(ies) and _____ as remainderman(men).

b. Under the terms of this trust (as provided by Section _____) the trust is to terminate:

☐ automatically, when _____, born _____, 19____ reaches the age of ____

☐ automatically, when the following event occurs: _____ This event occurred on _____, 19____ under the following circumstances: _____

☐ automatically, when a person entitled to demand invasion of the trust principal up to and including the remaining principal so demands. Such a demand was made by _____, a person so entitled, on _____, 19____.

☐ in my discretion, when the trust becomes economically infeasible to administer as such; it is now my opinion that continued trust administration is economically infeasible.

☐ in my discretion, when _____ becomes capable of managing his/her own property. I believe that he/she is now capable.

c. Therefore, I hereby terminate the trust, and pay over and assign all remaining trust principal and accumulated income to _____ as remainderman. This payment and assignment is absolutely free and clear.

d. The transfer is net of the sum of $_____ due to me as reasonable charges and expenses encountered in my capacity as trustee.

e. In witness to the above facts and circumstances, I have signed this statement on _____, 19____.

Signature:

Acknowledgment:

NOTE: If this instrument is recorded, local practice may call for appending the name and signature of the preparer.

TRUSTEES

CROSS-REFERENCE: See EXECUTORS: APPOINTMENT.

Bonding

1. (Not required) No trustee or successor trustee shall be required to post bond while acting under this trust instrument.

2. (Required of successor only) The trustee, while acting under this trust agreement, shall not be required to post bond. However, any successor trustee shall be required to post bond in an amount equal to or greater than the fair market value of the trust principal as of the time of the successor trustee's taking office.

3. (Required) Before beginning to serve as trustee, any trustee or successor trustee must obtain a bond payable to the trust estate, issued by an authorized surety company, as security for his/her/its faithful performance of duties under this trust agreement. The amount of the bond must be at least equal to the fair market value of the trust principal at the time of the application for the bond, plus one year's income assuming a rate of return of ____%.

    The trust itself will pay for the cost of the bond. The trustee has discretion to assign this payment either to principal or to income.

Compensation

1. (Minimum fee against percentage) The trustee shall be compensated for normal services at the annual rate of ____% of the fair market value of the trust assets, with a minimum annual fee of $_____. Furthermore, if the trust terminates within ____ years, the trustee will be entitled to receive the difference between $_____ and his/her/its total compensation over the life of the trust.

OR

(Trustee's fee schedule) For services rendered as executor/trustee, I direct that the _____ Trust Company be compensated in accordance with its schedule of fees, even if such fees are higher than the fiduciary's commissions specified by §____ of the Laws of the State of _____. Such compensation may be paid without prior approval of court.

NOTE: Some state laws (New Jersey's among them) require specific reference to statute when higher-than-statutory commissions are paid.

2. (Expenses) I direct the trustee to pay all expenses of trust administration (to be allocated between principal and income in the trustee's discretion). Such expenses include counsel fees and other costs necessary to protect the trust against challenges to its validity, and also include reasonable compensation for the trustee's services as trustee, all such amounts qualifying as a first lien on the trust estate.

Independence

1. (Renunciation by grantor) The grantor hereby renounces, both personally and for his/her estate, all vested, contingent, or reversionary right in trust principal or income. The grantor recognizes that he/she has no right to amend or revoke the trust or control the disposition of trust assets The grantor directs the trustee that no trust assets may ever be used to satisfy the grantor's legal obligations, to pay the premiums of policies on the grantor's life, or revert to the grantor or be used for his or her benefit.

Powers

1. (Investment) During the grantor's life the trustee is obliged to follow any written investment instructions given by the grantor, regardless of whether or not the investments so mandated are on the "legal list" or are considered suitably prudent investments for a fiduciary. The trustee will not be liable for any loss to the trust, or decline in value of trust assets, caused by good-faith compliance with the grantor's written instructions.

OR

In addition to the statutory powers, the trustee shall have the following powers as to all trust property:

- To subscribe for stocks and bonds
- To give proxies and participate in the merger, acquisition, or reorganization of any company whose securities are held by the trust
- To fix valuations of trust property, and to decide whether to make distributions in cash or in kind.

OR

The trustee may invest in any investment medium that might be chosen by a prudent and experienced investor whose goals were avoidance of speculation and maximization of trust income with preservation of capital.

2. (Borrowing) The trustee shall have the power to borrow on behalf of the trust, either on an unsecured basis or using trust property as collateral.

3. (Accounting) The trustee has an obligation to render an annual/quarterly/monthly account to the grantor during his/her lifetime, and to the income beneficiary subsequently, giving an account of trust receipts, disbursements, and income distributions. Such accounting is to be prepared using generally accepted accounting principles. If and when the person to whom the accounting is submitted approves it, the accounting will become final and binding on all persons as to all matters and transactions.

State Statute Chart

	Signature, Attestation	Witnesses	Self-Proof	Revocation	Interested Witnesses	Personal Property Letter	Incorporation by Reference	Elective Share	Pretermitted Spouse	Pretermitted Child	In Terrorem Clause
ALABAMA	43-8-131	43-8-131	43-8-132	43-8-136, -137			43-8-139	43-8-70	43-8-90	43-8-91	
ALASKA	13.11.155	13.11.155	13.11.165	13.11.180, -185	13.11.170	13.11.210	13.11.190	13.11.070	13.11.110	13.11.115	13.16.555
ARIZONA	14-2502	14-2502	14-2504	14-2507, -2508	14-2505	14-2513	14-2510	Community Property	14-2301	14-2302	
ARKANSAS	60-403	60-403	60-417	60-406, -407	60-402	60-419	60-418	60-501		60-507	
CALIFORNIA	Pro 6110	Pro 6110		Pro 6120-6122	Pro 6112		Pro 6130	Pro 120	Pro 6560	Pro 6570	Pro 372.5
COLORADO	15-11-502	15-11-502	15-11-504	15-11-507, -508	15-11-505	15-11-513	15-11-510	15-11-201	15-11-301	15-11-302	
CONNECTICUT	45-161	45-161	45-166	45-162	45-172			45-273a	45-162	45-162	
DELAWARE	T12§202	T12§202	T12§1305	T12§208, 209	T12§203	T12§212		T12§901	T12§321	T12§301	
D.C.	18-103	18-103		18-109	18-104			19-113		19-314	
FLORIDA	732.502	732.502	732.503	732.505 -.507	732.504	732.515	732.512	732.201	732.301	732.302	
GEORGIA	53-2-40	53-2-40	53-2-40.1	53-2-70 -76	53-2-45						53-2-107
HAWAII	560:2-502	560:2-502	560:2-504	560:2-507, -508	560:2-505	560:2-513	560:2-510	560:2-201			560:3-905
IDAHO	15-2-502	15-2-502	15-2-504	15-2-507, -508	15-2-505	15-2-513	15-2-510	15-2-203	15-2-301	15-2-302	15-3-905
ILLINOIS	ch 110½ §4-3	ch 110½ §4-3		ch 110½ §4-7	ch 110½ §4-6			ch 110½ §2-8		ch 110½ §4-10	
INDIANA	29-1-5-2	29-1-5-2	29-1-5-3	29-1-5-6-8	29-1-5-2			29-1-3-1		29-1-3-8	
IOWA	633.279(1)	633.279(1)	633.279(2)	633.271, .284	633.281	633.276		633.236		633.267	
KANSAS	59-606	59-606	59-606	56-610, -611	59-604	59-606		59-603			
KENTUCKY	394.060	394.040	394.225	394.080, .090,.092	394.210			392.080		394.460	
LOUISIANA	9:2442	9:2442		Art 1690-1696				CP		Art 1493-5	
MAINE	T18-A §2-502	T18-A §2-502	T18-A §2-504	T18-A §2-507, -508	T18A §2-505	T18A §2-513	T18A §2-510	T18-A §2-201	T18-A §2-301	T18-A §2-302	
MARYLAND	Est & T 4-102	Est & T 4-102		Est & T 4-105			Est & T 4-107	Est & T 3-203		Est & T 3-301	Est & T 4-413
MASS.	ch 191 §1	ch 191 §1		ch 191 §8,9	ch 191§2			ch 191§15		ch 191§20	
MICHIGAN	700.122	700.122		700.124	700.122	700.131a	700.130	700.281	700.126	700.127	700.168
MINNESOTA	524.2-502	524.2-502	524.2-504	524.2-507, -508	524.2-505	524.2-513	524.2-510	525.212		525.201	
MISSISSIPPI	91-5-1	91-5-1		91-5-3	91-5-9			91-5-27	91-5-27	91-5-5	
MISSOURI	474.320	474.320	474.337	474.400, .420	474.330	474.333		474.160	474.235	474.240	

	Adoptees	Illegitimates	Simultaneous Death	Pourover	Deposit of Will	Ante-Mortem Probate	Anti-Lapse	Estate Tax Apportionment	Abatement	Statutory Will
ALABAMA	43-8-48	43-8-230	43-7-1	43-8-140			43-8-224		43-8-76	
ALASKA	13.11.045	13.11.270	13.11.020	13.11.200	13.11.315		13.11.240	13.16.10	13.16.540	
ARIZONA	14-2109	14-2611	14-2804	14-2511	14-2901		14-2605		14-3902	
ARKANSAS	56-215	61-141	61-124	60-601	60-415	Laws 1979 act 194	60-410		62-2903, -2904	
CALIFORNIA	Pro 6152	Pro 6152	Pro 220	Pro 6300			Pro 6147	Pro 970	Pro 750, 751, 753	Pro 6220
COLORADO	15-11-109	15-11-611	15-11-613	15-11-511	15-11-901		15-11-605	15-12-916	15-12-902	
CONNECTICUT	45-64a,67	45-274	45-287	45-173a			45-176, -177		45-182	
DELAWARE	T12§508	T13§1303	T12§701				T12 §2313		T12 §2317	
D.C.		19-316, -318	19-501	18-306			18-308			
FLORIDA	732.108	732.108	732.601	732.513			732.604	733.817	733.805	
GEORGIA	19-8-14	53-4-4	53-11-1	53-14-1			53-2-103, -104	53-2-101 (a)	53-2-101 (b)	
HAWAII	560:2-611	560:2-611		560:2-511			560:2-605		560:3-902	
IDAHO	15-2-611	15-2-611	15-2-613	15-2-511			15-2-605, -606	15-3-916	15-3-902	
ILLINOIS	ch 110½ §2-4	ch 110½ §2-2	ch 110½ §3-1	ch 110½ §4-4			ch 110½ §4-11			
INDIANA	29-1-1-3, 29-1-2-8	29-1-2-5	29-2-14-1	29-1-6-1	29-1-6-1 (g)		29-1-17-4			
IOWA			633.523	633.275	633.286		633.273		633.436	
KANSAS	59-615		58-701	59-3101			59-615	79-1564 (d)	59-1405	
KENTUCKY			397.010	394.075	394.110		394.410		394.420, .450	
LOUISIANA	Art 214		Art 936					9:2431		
MAINE	T18-A §2-611	T18-A §2-611	T18-A §2-805	T18-A §2-511	2-901		T18-A §2-605	T18-A §3-916	T18-A §3-902	T18-A §2-514
MARYLAND	Est & T 1-205	Est & T 1-208	Cts & Jud Pro 10-801	Est & T 4-411, -412	Est & T 4-201		Est & T 4-403	Est & T 11-109	Est & T 9-103	
MASS.	ch 210 §8	ch 190§5	ch 190-A §1	ch 203 §3B	ch 191 §10		ch 191 §22	ch 191 §1A (6)	ch 191 §25	
MICHIGAN	700.128	700.138	720.101	555.461	700.142		700.134	730.11	700.157	
MINNESOTA	259.29	525.172	525.90	525.223	525.22		524.2-605	524.3-916	524.3-908	
MISSISSIPPI	93-17-13	91-1-15	91-3-1	91-5-11			91-5-7			
MISSOURI	453.090	474.060	471.010		474.510		474.460		473.620, .623, .637	

139

	Signature, Attestation	Witnesses	Self-Proof	Revocation	Interested Witnesses	Personal Property Letter	Incorporation by Reference	Elective Share	Pretermitted Spouse	Pretermitted Child	In Terrorem Clause
MONTANA	72-2-302	72-2-302	72-2-304	72-2-321--322	72-2-305	72-2-312	72-2-311	72-2-702	72-2-601	72-2-602	72-2-519
NEBRASKA	30-2327	30-2327	30-2329	30-2332, -2333	30-2330	30-2338	30-2335	30-2313	30-2320	30-2321	30-24, 103
NEVADA	133.040	133.040	133.050	133.110, .115, .120	133.060	133.045		Community Property		133.160, .170	
NEW HAMPSHIRE	551:2a	551:2a	551:2a	551:13, :14	551:3			560:10		551:10, :11	
NEW JERSEY	3B:3-2	3B:3-2	3B:3-4	3B:3-13, -14	3B:3-8	3B:3-11	3B:3-10	3B:8-1			3B:3-47
NEW MEXICO	45-2-502	45-2-502	45-2-504	45-2-507, -508	45-2-505	45-2-513	45-2-510	Community Property	45-2-301	45-2-302	45-3-916
NEW YORK	EPTL §3-2.1	EPTL §3-2.1		EPTL §3-4.1, 5-1.4	EPTL §3-3.2			EPTL §5-1.1		EPTL §§3-3.2	EPTL §3-3.5
N. CAROLINA	31-3.3	31-3.3	31-11-1	31-5.1 -5.7	31-10			30-1		31-5.5	
N. DAKOTA	30.1-08-02	30.1-08-02	30.1-08-04	30.1-08-07, -08	30.1-08-05	30.1-08-13	30.1-08-10	30.1-05-01	30.1-06-01	30.1-06-02	30.1-20-05
OHIO	2107.03	2107.03		2107.33	2107.15		2107.05	2107.39		2107.34	
OKLAHOMA	T84 §55	T84 §55	T84 §55	T84 §101, 114	T84 §143			T84 §44		T84 §131, 132-4	
OREGON	112.235	112.235		112.285, .305, .315	112.245			114.105		112.405	116.303
PENNSYLVANIA	20 §2502	20 §2502	20 §3132.1	20 §2505, 2507(2)				20 §2508	20 §2507	20 §2507	
RHODE ISLAND	33-5-5	33-5-5	33-7-26	33-5-9 -11	33-6-1			33-6-22		33-6-23	
S. CAROLINA	21-7-50	21-7-50	21-7-615	21-7-210, -230	21-7-690			21-5-710		21-7-450, 460	
S. DAKOTA	29-2-6	29-2-6	29-2-6-1	29-3-1-10	29-2-16,-17			30-5A-1		29-6-9 -12	
TENNESSEE	32-1-104	32-1-104		L1985 ch 139 §2	32-1-103			31-4-101		32-3-103	
TEXAS	Pro §59	Pro §59	Pro §59	Pro §63	Pro §61			Community Property		Pro §67	
UTAH	75-2-502	75-2-502	75-2-504	75-2-507, -508	75-2-505	75-2-513	75-2-510	75-2-201	75-2-301	75-2-302	75-3-905
VERMONT	T14 §5	T14 §5		T14 §11	T14 §10			T14 §402		T14 §555-557	
VIRGINIA	64.1-49	64.1-49	64.1-87.1, -87.2	64.1-58.1, -59	64.1-51			64.1-29	64.1-69.1	64.1-70, -71	
WASHINGTON	11.12.020	11.12.020	11.20.020	11.12.040, .050	11.12.160	11.12.260	11.12.255	Community Property	11.12.050	11.12.090	
W. VIRGINIA	41-1-3	41-1-3	41-5-15	41-1-6, -7	41-2-1			42-3-1		41-4-1, -2	
WISCONSIN	853.03	853.03		853.11	853.07(2)			861.05		853.25	
WYOMING	2-6-112	2-6-112	2-6-114	2-6-117, -118	2-6-112			2-5-101			

	Adoptees	Illegitimates	Simultaneous Death	Pourover	Deposit of Will	Ante-Mortem Probate	Anti-Lapse	Estate Tax Apportionment	Abatement	Statutory Will
MONTANA	72-2-503	72-2-503	72-2-205	72-2-314			72-2-512	72-16-601	72-3-901	
NEBRASKA	30-2309	30-2309	30-121; -2304	30-2336			30-2343		30-24,100	
NEVADA	127.160	126.041	135.010	163.220			133.200	150.290	148.030	
NEW HAMPSHIRE	170B:20	561:4	563:1	563-A:1			551:12		561:18	
NEW JERSEY	3B:3-48	3B:3-48	3B:6-1	3B:4-1			3B:3-35			
NEW MEXICO	45-2-611	45-2-611	45-8-1	46-5-1	45-2-901		45-2-605		45-3-902	
NEW YORK	EPTL §2-1.3	EPTL §4-1.2	EPTL §2-1.6	EPTL §3-3.7			EPTL §3-3.3	EPTL §2-1.8	EPTL §13-1.3	
N. CAROLINA	48-23	31-5.5	28A-24.1	31-47	31-11		31-42		28A-15.5	
N. DAKOTA	30.1-04-09	30.1-04-09	31-12-01	30.1-08-11		30.1-08.1-01-04	30.1-09-05	30.1-20-16	30.1-20-02	
OHIO	3107.15	2105.17	2105.21	2107.63	2107.07	2107.081	2107.52		2107.54, .55	
OKLAHOMA	T10 §60-16	T84 §215	T58 §1001	T84 §301	T84 §81-3		T84 §142		T84 §8	
OREGON	112.175	112.105	112.575	112.265			112.395		116.133	
PENNSYLVANIA	20 §2514	20 §2514	20 §8501	20 §2515			20 §2514 (9)-(11)	20 §2514, (15)	20 §3541, 3542	
RHODE ISLAND	15-7-16	33-1-8	33-2-1		33-7-1		33-6-19, -20			
S. CAROLINA	20-7-1770	21-3-30	21-9-20	21-33-10			21-7-470			
S. DAKOTA	25-6-16	29-1-15	29-8-1	29-2-18	29-4-1		29-6-8	29-7-1	29-6-16	
TENNESSEE			31-3-101	32-3-106	32-1-112		32-3-104, -105	30-2-614		
TEXAS	Pro §40	Pro §42	Pro §47	Pro §58a	Pro §71		Pro §68		Pro §321	
UTAH	75-2-611	75-2-611	75-2-1001	75-2-1001	75-2-901		75-2-605	75-3-916	75-3-902	
VERMONT	T15 §448	T14 §553	T14 §621	T14 §2329	T14 §2		T14 §558			
VIRGINIA	64.1-71.1	64.1-71.1	64.1-97	64.1-73	64.1-56		64.1-64.1	64.1-161		
WASHINGTON	11.04.085	11.04.081	11.05.010	11.12.250			11.12.110			
W. VIRGINIA	48-4-11	42-1-5	42-5-1	41-3-8			41-3-3			
WISCONSIN	851.51	851.13	851.55		853-09		853.27		863.11	853.50-.62
WYOMING	2-4-107	2-4-102	2-13-101	2-6-103			2-6-106		2-7-808	

Table of Cases

Revocation

Bloomer v. Capps, 620 SW2d 365 (Mo.Sup. 1981)

Clymer v. Mayo, 393 Mass. 754, 473 NE2d 1084 (Mass. 1985)

Matter of Foundas' Estate, 112 Misc.2d 973, 448 NYS2d 114 (1982)

Estate of Haurin, 43 Colo. App. 279, 605 P2d 65 (1979)

Life Insurance Co. of North America v. Cassidy, 35 Cal.3d 599, 200 Cal.Rptr. 28, 676 P2d 1050 (1984)

Mailey Trust, 20 Fiduciary Reporter 597 (Pa. 1970)

Miller v. First National Bank & Trust Co., 637 P2d 75 (Okla. Sup. 1981)

Re Estate of Perigen, 653 SW2d 717 (1983)

Sedberry v. Johnson, 62 NC App.425, 302 SE2d 924 (1983)

In re Thompson's Estate, 214 Neb. 899, 336 NW2d 590 (1983)

Will Formalities

Matter of Agar, NYLJ 7/1/82 p. 5

Succession of Augustus, 441 So.2d 730 (La. 1984)

Backlund Will, 30 Fiduciary Rep. 141 (Pa. 1980)

Succession of Brown, 458 So2d 140 (La. 1984)

In re Camin's Estate, 212 Neb. 490, 323 NW2d 827 (1982)

Matter of Estate of Cornelius, 80 Ill.Dec. 687, 465 NE2d 1033 (1984)

In re Cutsinger, 445 P2d 778 (Okla. 1968)

Davis v. Davis, 471 A2d 1008 (DC 1984)

Re Davis' Estate, 438 So2d 543 (Fla. App. 1983)

Matter of Dodson's Estate, 119 Mich.App. 427, 326 NW2d 532 (1982)

Dorfman v. Allen, 386 Mass. 121, 434 NE2d 1012 (1982)

Douthit v. McLeroy, 539 SW2d 351 (Tex. 1976)

In re Estate of Flicker, 215 Neb. 495, 339 NW2d 914 (1983)

In re Flider's Estate, 213 Neb. 153, 328 NW2d 197 (1982)

Gilbert v. Gilbert, 652 SW2d 663 (Ky.App. 1983)

Matter of Hall, 118 Misc.2d 1052, 462 NYS2d 154 (1983)

Matter of Hughson, 97 Misc.2d 427, 411 NYS2d 839 (1978)

In re Johnson's Estate, 359 So2d 425 (Fla. 1978)

Will of Keane, 99 Misc.2d 714, 417 NYS2d 28 (1979)

Matter of Kelly's Estate, 99 NM 482, 660 P2d 124 (1983)

Estate of Lewis, NYLJ 11/1/79 p. 11

Limits on Testamentary Freedom

Estate of Powers, 117 Ill.App.3d 1087, 73 Ill.D. 524, 454 NE2d 384 (1983)

Roberts v. Estate of Roberts, 664 SW2d 634 (Mo. 1984)

Rosenberg v. Lipnick, 383 NE2d 385 (Mass.Sup.Jud.Ct. 1979)

Estate of Schwartz, 405 NYS2d 920, 94 Misc.2d 1024 (1978), aff'd 413 NYS2d 1023

Sheffield v. Scott, 620 SW2d 691 (Tex. 1981)

Smith v. Crook, 160 Cal.App.3d 245, 206 Cal.Rptr. 524 (1984)

Solomon v. Dunlap, 372 So2d 218 (Fla.App. 1979)

Topper v. Stewart, 449 So2d 373 (Fla. 1984)

Matter of Estate of Westfahl, 675 P2d 21 (Okla. 1983)

Wojtalewicz v. Waitel, 93 Ill.App.3d 1061, 418 NE2d 418 (1981)

Matter of Estate of Zarrow, 688 P2d 47 (1984)

Special Drafting Problems

Auric v. Continental Casualty Co., 111 Wis.2d 507, 331 NW2d 325 (1983)

In re Estate of Baker, 495 Pa. 528, 434 A2d 1213 (1981)

In re Estate of Barker, 448 So2d 28 (Fla. 1984)

Baxley v. Birmingham Trust Nat'l Bank, 334 So2d 848 (Ala. 1976)

Estate of Becker, NYLJ 7/16/79 p. 15

Matter of Estate of Boldt, 342 NW2d 463 (Ia. 1983)

Bucquet v. Livingston, 57 Cal.App.3d 914, 129 Cal.Rptr. 514 (1976)

In re Cancik, 106 Ill.2d 11, 87 Ill.Dec. 36, 476 NE2d 738 (1985)

Chicago Title & Trust v. Schwartz, 120 Ill.App.3d 324, 458 NE2d 151 (1983)

In re Criss' Trust, 213 Neb. 379, 329 NW2d 842 (1983)

Estate of Cunningham, NYLJ 5/12/75 p. 16

Davis v. Davis, 471 A2d 1008 (D.C. 1984)

Re Estate of Deardoff, 10 Oh.St.3d 108, 461 NE2d 1292 (1984)

Estate of Douglas, NYLJ 4/9/80 p. 12

Evans v. McCoy, 291 Md. 562, 436 A2d 436 (1981)

Estate of Farone, NYLJ 5/10/85 p. 1

Favata v. Rosenberg, 106 Ill.App.3d 572, 62 Ill.Dec. 467, 436 NE2d 49 (1982)

Gadoury v. Caldwell, 425 So2d 220 (Fla. 1983)

Matter of Geis' Estate, 132 Ariz. 350, 645 P2d 1264 (1982)

Matter of Estate of Giacomini, 4 Kan.App.2d 126, 603 P2d 218 (1979)

In re Estate of Graham, 4 Ariz.App. 193, 419 P2d 97 (1966)

Griffin v. Gould, 104 Ill.App.3d 397, 60 Ill.Dec. 132, 432 NE2d 1031 (1982)

Guy v. Liederbach, 279 Pa.Super.543, 421 A2d 333 (1981)

Matter of Estate of Hall, 118 Misc.2d 1052, 462 NYS2d 154 (1983)

Re Estate of Hannon, 447 So2d 1027 (Fla.App. 1984)

Heyer v. Flaig, 70 Cal.2d 223, 74 Cal.Rptr. 225, 449 P2d 161 (1969)

Estate of Hirschi, 113 Cal.App.3d 681, 170 Cal.Rptr. 186 (1980)

Succession of Kearl, 440 So2d 179 (La. 1983)

Lamb Estate, 445 Pa. 323, 285 A2d 163 (1973)

Landstrom v. Krettler, 105 Ill.App.3d 863, 61 Ill.Dec. 660, 435 NE2d 149 (1982)

Lehman v. Corpus Christi Nat'l Bank, 668 SW2d 687 (Tex. 1984)

Licata v. Spector, 26 Ct.Sup. 378, 255 A2d 28 (1966)

Lucas v. Hamm, 56 Cal.2d. 583, 15 Cal.Rptr. 821, 364 P2d 685 (1961), cert.den. 368 U.S. 987

Maneri v. Amodeo, 38 Misc.2d 190, 238 NYS2d 302 (1963)

In re Macfarlane's Estate, 313 Pa.Super. 397, 459 A2d 1289 (1983)

Martin v. First National Bank of Mobile, 412 So2d 250 (Ala. 1982)

McAbee v. Edwards, 340 So2d 1165 (Fla. 1976)

In re Estate of McGlone, 436 So2d 441 (1983)

Millwright v. Romer, 322 NW2d 30 (Ia. 1982)

Odom v. Odom, 238 Ga. 733, 235 SE2d 29 (1977)

Ogle v. Fuiten, 112 Ill.App.2d 1048, 68 Ill.Dec. 491, 445 NE2d 1344 (1983), aff'd 446 NE2d 224

In re Estate of Pedrick, 505 Pa. 571, 482 A2d 215 (1984)

In re Disciplinary Action Against Prueter, 359 NW2d 613 (Minn.Sup. 1984)

Estate of Riley, 498 Pa. 395, 446 A2d 903 (1982)

Matter of Ross, 102 Misc.2d 796, 424 NYS2d 661 (1980)

Matter of Estate of Rudy, 329 Pa.Super. 477, 478 A2d 879 (1984)

Sandy v. Mohout, 1 Oh.St.3d 143, 438 NE2d 117 (1982)

Estate of Scheer, NYLJ 10/16/80 p. 12

Matter of Schmidt's Estate, 638 P2d 809 (Colo. 1981)

Silverthorn v. Jennings, 620 SW2d 894 (Tex. 1981)

Skoog v. Fredell, 332 NW2d 333 (Ia. 1983)

Stowe v. Smith, 184 Ct. 194, 441 A2d 81 (1981)

Estate of Strauss, NYLJ 8/27/82 p. 7

In re Conduct of Tonkon, 642 P2d 660 (Ore. Sup. 1982)

Estate of Tower, 323 Pa.Sup. 232, 470 A2d 568 (1983), aff'd 487 A2d 820

Vicars v. Mullins, 227 Va. 432, 318 SE2d 377 (Va. 1984)

Matter of Waskawic, NYLJ 1/17/80 p. 16

Wlk v. Wlk, 681 P2d 336 (Alaska 1984)

Woodfork v. Sanders, 248 So2d 419 (La.App. 1981)

Substantive Issues

Estate of Bernstrauch, 210 Neb. 135, 313 NW2d 264 (1981)

In re Blakey's Estate, 363 So2d 630 (Fla. 1978)

In re Estate of Britt, 112 Ill.App.3d 186, 67 Ill.Dec. 952, 445 NE2d 367 (1983)

Matter of Brown's Estate, 230 Kan. 697, 640 P2d 1250 (1982)

Succession of Catanzaro, 417 So2d 863 (La. 1982)

Matter of Congdon's Estate, 309 NW2d 261 (Minn. 1982)

Trusts

Bibliography

BOOKS

Casner, A. James, *Estate Planning* (5th ed.). Boston, Massachusetts: Little, Brown, 1984.

Friedman, Suri, Publ. Mgr., 1G, 1H *Bender's Forms for the Consolidated Laws of the State of New York Annotated.* New York, New York: Matthew Bender, 1983 (1985 pocket part).

Kess, Sidney, and Bert Westlin, *Financial and Estate Planning.* Chicago, Illinois: Commerce Clearing House (looseleaf service).

Klipstein, Harold, *Drafting New York Wills: Laws and Forms.* New York, New York: Matthew Bender, 1985.

Lawyers' Co-Op Publishing Co. *3, 4 New Jersey Forms* §§24:1–26:108 Rochester, New York: Lawyer's Co-Op Publishing Co., 1984.

Moore, Malcolm, Chairman, *Use of Trusts in Estate Planning 1985.* New York, New York: Practicing Law Institute, 1985 (Estate Planning and Administration Handbook Series #160).

Parella, Robert and Joel Miller, *Modern Trust Forms and Checklists with Commentary,* Boston, Massachusetts: Warren Gorham & Lamont, 1980 (1985 supplement).

Rabkin, Jacob, and Mark Johnson, 3,4 *Current Legal Forms with Tax Analysis.* New York, New York: Matthew Bender, 1985.

Shaffer, Thomas, *Death, Property and Lawyers: A Behavioral Approach.* Indianapolis, Indiana: Dunellen Pub. Co., 1970.

Shaffer, Thomas, *The Planning and Drafting of Wills and Trusts.* Albany, New York: Foundation Press, 1972.

Susman, Gerald, *Estate Planning.* New York, New York: Law Journal Seminars-Press, 1981 (1984, 1985 updates).

ARTICLES AND ANNOTATIONS

Aresty & Vacovec, "Automating the Estate Planning Practice," 43 Inst. on Federal Tax 58 (29) (1985).

Brosterhous, "Conflicts of Interest in Estate Planning and Administration," 123 Trusts and Estates 18 (1984).

Comment, "A Risk in Wills: Standard of Care Gets Tighter," 70 A.B.A. J. 41 (1984).

Comment, "Death Tax Clauses in Wills and Trusts: Discussion and Sample Clauses," 19 Real Property Probate & Trust J. 495 (1984).

Comment, "Estate Practice in the Office of the Future," 19 Real Property Probate & Trust J. 721 (1984).

Committee on Planning and Drafting: Administrative Provisions, "Death Tax Clauses in Wills and Trusts: Discussion and Sample Clauses," 19 Real Property Probate & Trust J. 495 (1984).

Corn, "The Rights of Adopted-Out Persons," New York Law Journal November 25, 1985 p. 1.

Friday, "Conflicts of Interest When an Attorney Drafts a Will Which Names Him as a Beneficiary," 9 J. Legal Profession 175 (1984).

Grant, "A Videowill: Safe and Sure," 70 A.B.A. J. 86 (1984).

Hoban, "Lawyers of the Future: A Mild Form of Artificial Intelligence," 13 Student Lawyer 8 (1984).

Hodge, "Drafting Attorney's Liability to Intended Beneficiaries of a Will," 18 Val. U. L. Rev. 119 (1983).

Houghton, "Computer Programs for Probate Lawyers," 57 New York State B. J. 15 (1985).

Huff, "Spendthrift Clauses: Legality and Effect on Post-Transfer Estate Planning," 18 Inst. on Estate Planning 12-1(42) (1984).

Johns, "Federal Income Tax Aspects of Will Clauses," 16 Tax Adviser 27 (1985).

Johnson, "Word 'Child' or 'Chiidren' in Will as Including Grandchild or Grand-children," 30 ALR 4th 319 (1984).

Johnston, "Legal Malpractice in Estate Planning—Perilous Times Ahead for the Practitioner," 67 Iowa L. Rev. 629 (1982).

Kraut, "Right of Heir or Devisee to Have Realty Exonerated from Lien Thereof at the Expense of Personal Estate," 4 ALR 3d 1023 (1965 plus current supplement).

Mann, "Self-Proving Affidavits and Formalism in Wills Adjudication," 63 Wash. U. L. Q. 39 (1985).

Miller, "Creating an Estate Plan Data Base," 124 Trusts & Estates 46 (1985).

Mooney & Henry, "Charitable Giving Techniques for Business Owners," 123 Trusts & Estates 25 (1984).

Mortland, "Will and Trust Provisions Concerning Former Spouses, Adopted Children, and Spendthrift Clauses are Construed," 12 Estate Planning 248 (1985).

Pedrick, "How to be Happy in Estate Planning," 18 Inst. on Estate Planning, 21-1(27) (1984).

Russ, "Right of Illegitimate Grandchildren to Take Under Testamentary Gift to 'Grandchildren'", 17 ALR 4th 1293 (1982 plus current supplement).

Schneider, "Self-Proved Wills—a Trap for the Unwary," 8 Northern Kentucky L. Rev. 539 (1981).

Stewart, "Estate Planning and Will Drafting: Suggestions," 18 Ark. Lawyer 54 (1984).

Squires & Muckestone, "A Simple 'Simple' Will," 57 Wash. L. Rev. 461 (1982).

Thomason, "How Estate Planners Can Cope with the Increasing Risk of Malpractice Claims," 12 Estate Planning 130 (1985).

Index